How To Study The Word

Taking the Bible From the Pages To the Heart

From Lee Andrews
To: Dave Johnson
'05

How To Study The Word

Taking the Bible From the Pages To the Heart

Terry Lawson

Unless otherwise indicated, all Scripture quotations in this volume are from the *King James Version* of the Bible.

First Printing 1999

ISBN 0-89276-959-9

In the U.S. write:
Kenneth Hagin
Ministries
P.O. Box 50126
Tulsa, OK 74150-0126

In Canada write:
Kenneth Hagin Ministries
P.O. Box 335, Station D
Etobicoke (Toronto), Ontario
Canada, M9A 4X3

Contents

Introduction

The purpose of this book is to help you see more of the riches that Jesus has provided for you and to share with you, not a doctrine about Jesus, but Jesus Himself. Studying the Word of God is no intellectual study. In fact, if you read the first three chapters of First Corinthians, you will find such statements as, "... *the foolishness of God is wiser than men* ..." (1 Cor. 1:25); "... *we preach Christ crucified* ... *unto the Greeks* [Gentiles] *foolishness*" (v. 23); "... *your faith should not stand in the wisdom of men* ..." (1 Cor. 2:5); and "... *the wisdom of this world is foolishness with God* ..." (1 Cor. 3:19). T. Austin-Sparks in his book, *The Centrality and Universality of the Cross,*[1] makes the following statement: "Man believes that he is all the time improving, when, as a matter of fact, there is no moral elevation corresponding to the intellectual development."

In our culture we have developed our intellect at the expense of our spirits. We have great centers and schools where we can go to develop our bodies, and large universities where we spend millions of dollars for the development of our minds, our intellect and emotions. There is big business in the development of the body and soul, but the spirit of man is often neglected. When someone points out the need to cultivate the human spirit, often that person is said to be either a fanatic or too religious.

One scientist wrote: "Both history and science give us warrant for believing that humanity has made great advances in accumulating knowledge and experience and in devising instruments of living, and the value of all these is indisputable. But they do not constitute real progress in human nature itself, and in the absence of such progress those gains are external, precarious, and liable to be turned to our own destruction."

Surely we can see that there is more wisdom in God's foolishness than in men's cleverness! In this book I am endeavoring to enable you to learn to feed yourself — to feed your inner man, your spirit. It is like the old saying, "If you give a man a fish you have fed him a meal, but teach that man to fish and you feed him for a lifetime."

This is not to say that once you learn to feed your spirit, you will not have to go to church as often. That is the thinking of an unrenewed mind. The more you actually feed your spirit, the more you will want to be in church. D. L. Moody, speaking on the subject of Bible study, once said: "The quicker you learn to feed yourself the better. I pity down in my heart any men and women who have been attending some church for say five, ten, or twenty years, and yet have not learned to feed themselves." He goes on to say: "Read the Bible itself — do not spend all your time on commentaries and helps. If a man spent all his time reading up the chemical constituents of bread and milk, he would soon starve."

Pay close attention to what you choose to read. It is all too easy to use commentaries and study helps in place of actually reading your Bible. It is easier to read *about* the Bible than to read the Bible itself, just like it is easier to talk *about* God than to talk with God.

Take notes in your Bible and underline scriptures that speak to you. This way you will be making your own commentary. Then when you reread that part, you will receive again the blessing you had before. It will bring the Word of God closer to you. Also have an unmarked copy that you can read. This way you will read all the Scripture, not only what you have highlighted.

Remember, the Bible is your operator's manual, as one writer has put it. Your Bible is your well to the water of Life.

You need to use it daily. Your Bible contains the food your spirit needs to feed on to cause it to grow. Nothing else will take the place of your Bible. Listening to the Word being preached and taught is very important to your personal development. Reading through your Bible by reading it daily will help you greatly in your spiritual growth. You need to include both hearing the Word preached and reading the Word daily in your spiritual life. These things should not be left out. But they will not take the place of you yourself feeding upon the Word.

Reading God's Word and feeding upon God's Word are two different things. By learning to use the study tools described in this book that only scholars could use until a few years ago, you can prepare a diet of God's Word that will substantially enrich your life.

Once you have prepared a *meal* of God's Word, you need to EAT IT! Spend time with it. After a while, you will think that feeding on the Word takes too long and that you do not have time for it. However, I have found that if you do not spend the time you should studying and eating God's Word, then the devil will come and take even more of your time at a later date.

For instance, if you do not feed on scriptures pertaining to healing for you and your family, then you are open for an attack of the devil. He will come and cause you to spend time nursing yourself or your family back to health. He steals time (not to mention money) from you, even to the point, perhaps, of you having to miss church services, thus missing the blessing that God has for you there.

Whether it is finances, worry, knowing who you are in Christ, or any other area of your life, the same principle holds true. Bible study, feeding on God's Word, then applying it to your life will put you on your way to receiving God's supply of abundant blessings to meet all your needs.

Remember, this is a progressive walk.

---

[1] *The Centrality and Universality of the Cross.* (Washington, D.C.: Testimony Book Ministry, n.d.)

Part I

How To Study the Bible

Chapter 1
Why Study the Bible?

You know, it is always regarded a great event in the family when a child can feed itself. It is propped up at the table, and at first perhaps it uses the spoon upside down, but by and by it uses it all right, and mother, or perhaps sister, claps her hands and says, "Just see, baby's feeding himself!" Well, what we need as Christians is to be able to feed ourselves.

— *D. L. Moody*[1]

Every Christian begins his new life in Christ as a baby, fresh and new and vulnerable. And, like a baby, ready to eat. New Christians are eager to learn and ready to grow. But, like new babies, they are not born knowing how to feed themselves. Even if they could feed themselves, they would not know which foods are healthy for them to eat. They do not know which foods will cause them to grow and thrive and give them energy and strength.

Perhaps this explains why many baby Christians, most of them hungry for spiritual nourishment, become deceived by cults, or more often, "blown about by every wind of doctrine." (Eph. 4:14). I am sure we all know Christians like this, always following after every new doctrine or searching for some *new* teaching, the latest and *hottest* revelation. They run from one meeting to the next, hoping to finally get set free, not realizing that all the while the answer (the Bible) is right on their shelf. Unfortunately, since they do not become rooted and grounded in God's Word, many end up confused, even dropping out of church entirely. The sad part is that few of these brothers or sisters ever spent any real time in God's Word, finding God's plan for their lives.

Perhaps one reason why so many who desire to study God's Word do not is that they just simply do not know how to go about it. Many sincere Bible students are intimidated by all the study tools available, not knowing which ones would be helpful to them, or even if they would be able to use them at all. They may feel overwhelmed by the prospect of studying so large a book as the Bible, with all its complexities and hard-to-understand passages. The Apostle Peter himself said that there are ". . .*some things hard to be understood, which they that are unlearned and unstable wrest, as they do also the other scriptures, unto their own destruction*" (2 Peter 3:16).

Such *unlearned and unstable* men, pretending to be learned, often preach error, and many are deceived by them. It is easy to see the importance of learning how to study God's Word for ourselves.

We study the Bible for spiritual and moral strength. In our study, we should never allow ourselves the liberty to prove a point for the point's sake. We should not allow our situation to interpret the Word of God, but rather let the Word of God interpret our situation.

Some may say that healing is not for us today because they see sickness in their life, yet the Word of God declares that by the stripes of Jesus we are healed (1 Peter 2:24). To interpret that healing is no longer for us today is to take sides against God's Word. God requires that we take the time to know what His Word says.

If we know Gods Word, then we know God's will. Allow integrity to prevail as you seek God's Word. If you find something there that says you need to change the way you are living, then change it. This is, to a great degree, what the Holy Spirit was saying through the Apostle Paul in his letter to the

Philippians, when he said, *". . . work out your own salvation with fear and trembling"* (Phil. 2:12). This is a working out from spirit to soul to body. Therefore, get God's Word in your spirit, allowing it to work in you and be your source of spiritual development.

Knowing God Through His Word

Throughout time men have sought to understand the Bible. Great scholars have struggled with its truths, while at the same time, others with no formal training or religious background have, with the help of the Holy Spirit, gleaned great wisdom from its pages. God's Word is not to be understood with the intellect, but rather grasped by the spirit of man.

God has preserved His Word through the ages of time. Many dear, dedicated Christians have given their lives in order that we may have this precious gift of God's Word. We are a blessed generation. Bibles are plenteous, even in many of the previously unreachable communist countries. Past generations have yearned and prayed for the blessing we often take so lightly.

The study of God's Word is a privilege, given by God Himself. Yet too many of us do not take advantage of the vast wealth of wisdom and help for living that are found in its pages. We are often all too content to let someone else, our pastor or Bible teacher for example, do all the studying for us. (After all, isn't that what we pay them for?) We all too often settle for a thirty-minute sermon once or twice or even three times a week as the main source of our spiritual nourishment.

Yet the Bible is the single most important book a Christian can own. It is his sword against the attacks of the enemy. *"And take . . . the sword of the Spirit, which is the word of God"* (Eph. 6:17). Yes, the Word is our sword, but a sword is no good to a soldier if he does not take it out and use it. Even more than that, it is not enough only to use it, but to win his battle he must know *how* to use it.

Knowing how to use God's Word is vital to our spiritual growth. Not only is God's Word our sword against the enemy, but it is important for all areas of our life. It is our encouragement, our enlightenment, our strength. Its words fill us with peace, with courage, and give us knowledge and understanding. In its pages are found the history of the world, how God created the heavens and the earth, and how He knows each of us, even numbering the hairs on our heads. The plan of salvation is found there, also healing and the message of freedom.

The life and works of our precious Lord Jesus are found therein, and the letters give us instructions on how to live our lives in a manner pleasing to Him. God's Word should be the center of every area of our lives, for God and His Word are one and the same.

It is through God's Word that we come to know Him, who He is and what He wants to communicate to us His people. Through God's Word we gain knowledge of Him. There are many in this world who seek after knowledge. Many in the church, too, seem consumed with this search for knowledge, collecting many volumes and pouring over them, searching for some new tidbit of information. But what we must always remember is that we are not striving for knowledge for the sake of knowledge, but rather we are striving to know God.

Webster's New International Dictionary of the English Language (Second Edition) defines *knowledge* as "familiarity gained by actual experience . . . technical acquaintance; as a knowledge of life." *Webster's New Collegiate Dictionary* calls it "the fact or condition of knowing something with familiarity gained through experience or association." In other words, knowledge simply means having a relationship with someone or something. It is to the development of this relationship that this book is dedicated.

Let's look at a familiar verse of Scripture:

HOSEA 4:6
6   My people are destroyed for lack of knowledge. . . .

J. W. Povah translates Hosea 4:6 as: "Destroy! My people have let you destroy them because they do not know Me. . . ."

Notice the way that *knowledge* is rendered *know* in the above passage. This is a very familiar but very misunderstood passage. Keep it in mind as we look at some more passages.

GENESIS 4:1
1   And Adam knew Eve his wife; and she con-ceived, and bare Cain, and said, I have gotten a man from the Lord.

The word *knew* in this passage is the root word for the word *knowledge* (the same word used in Hosea 4:6 — Strong's #3045). Notice that this word *knew* in Genesis 4:6 is referring to a relationship between Adam and Eve, in this case an intimate relationship.

LUKE 1:34
34 Then said Mary unto the angel, How shall this be, seeing I know not a man?

Here again, the word *know* is referring to a relationship. God's people are destroyed for a lack of relationship with Him.

JOHN 17:3
3   And this is life eternal, that they might know thee the only true God, and Jesus Christ, whom thou hast sent.

Now let's look at this verse in two more translations:

> **JOHN 17:3** (*Amplified*)
> And this is eternal life: [it means] to know (to perceive, recognize, become acquainted with, and understand) You, the only true and real God, and [likewise] to know Him, Jesus [as the] Christ (the Anointed One, the Messiah), Whom You have sent.

> **JOHN 17:3** (*Baxter*)
> And what is life eternal, but that perfect knowledge of thee, which fills the soul with love and joy, and knowledge of thy glory, shining forth in thy Son Jesus Christ with his body the heavenly society. And the beginning of this knowledge is the beginning and way to perfection.

Jesus said that eternal life is knowing the Father. This is the kind of knowledge we must seek after in our daily study of God's Word.

What Is Bible Study?

Hard Work

Bible study, first of all, is not the pain and torture that many people believe it to be. Although it takes a certain amount of work and discipline, it can be, along with prayer, the most rewarding part of your day. Sometimes in our study of the Bible, we are like a chef preparing a meal. Often after all the time and effort spent preparing it, he seldom if ever gets to eat any of it.

After you have gleaned and gathered from the Word of God, along with your commentaries, dictionaries, word study books, and notes from Sunday service, be sure to eat the meal that you have prepared. Remember, you can eat many times from one meal. Realize that God's Word is forever settled in heaven and is the same yesterday, today, and forever. The preparation you did last year is still pertinent for you today.

Let's look at Second Timothy 2:6 in a few translations.

2 TIMOTHY 2:6 (*New Life*)
A hard-working farmer should receive first some of what he gathers from the field.

2 TIMOTHY 2:6 (*Peterson*)
It's the diligent farmer who gets the produce.

2 TIMOTHY 2:6 (*Pyle*)
You know too, the husbandman labours in tilling, sowing, or planting his ground a considerable time, before he can expect to reap the crop.

During the gold rush in America when a person went out to mine for gold, as soon as he found a small nugget or other evidence of gold, he would immediately unload his pack animal in that location and start digging. This is the way that one should study the Word of God. When you find a special nugget, stop there and begin digging. You will find a vast treasure lies just below the surface.

Discipline

Discipline is necessary if we are to be serious students of the Bible. It is important to set up a regimen for study and stick to it. Do not, however, allow a season of laxness in your Bible study to become an excuse not to pick it back up again. Too often we think, "I've already missed several days in a row, so what's the use in doing it now?" That is exactly what the devil would like for you to think. I imagine that if you missed several meals in a row that you would not apply this principle.

These verses show us the importance of discipline in our study of God's Word:

> **PSALM 119:31**
> **31 I have stuck unto thy testimonies: O Lord, put me not to shame.**

> **2 TIMOTHY 2:15**
> **15 Study to shew thyself approved unto God, a workman that needeth not to be ashamed, rightly dividing the word of truth.**

Dave

> **2 TIMOTHY 2:15 (*Williams*)**
> **Do your best to present yourself to God an approved workman who has nothing to be ashamed of, who properly presents the message of truth.**

Joy

More than hard work and discipline, Bible study should be a joy. There is great joy in reading and studying God's Word, and great joy in the relationship with the Lord that develops as we spend time in His Word. There must be a continual feeding upon the Word of God to maintain this joy.

The Bible tells us much about the joy to be found in the study of God's Word. Here are just a few examples:

> **PSALM 19:8**
> **8   The statutes of the Lord are right, rejoicing the heart: the commandment of the Lord is pure, enlightening the eyes.**

> **PSALM 19:8 (*The Living Bible*)**
> **God's laws are perfect. They protect us, make us wise, and give us joy and light.**

Jeremiah 15:16 tells us that there is both joy and rejoicing found in our hearts when we *eat* the Word of God. If you are wondering where your joy has gone, begin to open up your Bible and let it fill you with His joy!

JEREMIAH 15:16
16 Thy words were found, and I did eat them; and thy word was unto me the joy and rejoicing of mine heart: for I am called by thy name, O Lord God of hosts.

JEREMIAH 15:16 (*Spurrell*)
Thy words were found, and I devoured them, and Thy words were unto me the joy and rejoicing of my heart; because I am called by Thy name, O Jehovah God of hosts.

What Are the Rewards of Bible Study?

PSALM 1:1-3
1 Blessed is the man that walketh not in the counsel of the ungodly, nor standeth in the way of sinners, nor sitteth in the seat of the scornful.
2 But his delight is in the law of the Lord; and in his law doth he meditate day and night.
3 And he shall be like a tree planted by the rivers of water, that bringeth forth his fruit in his season; his leaf also shall not wither; and whatsoever he doeth shall prosper.

What a beautiful and wonderful promise God has given! If we, first, shall not walk in the ways of worldly men, and, second, shall delight ourselves in God's law and meditate therein day and night, then we shall be like trees planted by rivers of water, bringing forth fruit in season. Our leaves shall not whither, and whatsoever we do shall prosper! In other words, diligent Bible study with a humble and obedient heart toward God will cause us to become like well watered trees, not only strong but fruitful as well, watered by the stream that flows from the throne of God. And God has promised that if we will put His Word first, we will prosper in everything we do.

We find this same promise again in the first chapter of Joshua:

> **JOSHUA 1:8**
> **8   This book of the law shall not depart out of thy mouth; but thou shalt meditate therein day and night, that thou mayest observe to do according to all that is written therein: for then thou shalt make thy way prosperous, and then thou shalt have good success.**

To be prosperous in God's sense means more than being wealthy. Remember in Psalm 1:3 it says that whatsoever we do shall prosper. This means that all areas of life, all troubles and temptations and struggles, fall under this promise to the student of God's Word. E. W. Kenyon translates the last part of Joshua 1:8 as, ". . . you will be able to deal wisely in the affairs of life."

Remember that God rewards those who diligently seek Him (Heb. 11:6). The rewards of Bible study are many and rich. If we diligently seek the Lord, our reward will come from Him. And His rewards are out of this world! God's rewards are both temporal and eternal. Jesus said, "If you abide in Me, and My words abide in you, you will ask what you desire, and it shall be done for you" (John 15:7).

Another reward of Bible study that the Scriptures point out is peace.

> **PSALM 119:165**
> **165 Great peace have they which love thy law: and nothing shall offend them.**

The study of God's Word brings peace to our lives. If we are truly rooted and grounded in God's Word, nothing will be able to shake us or disturb our peace. We will not be easily offended by others.

The best reward of Bible study is, however, the development of our relationship with the Lord. This is the very heart of Christianity. D. L. Moody once said, "In our prayers we talk to God, in our Bible study God talks to us, and we had better let God do most of the talking." It is through the study of God's Word that we come to know Him for He reveals Himself, with the help of the Holy Spirit, to our hearts through the Scriptures. The more you love God's Word, the stronger your faith will grow.

Finally, Bible study produces wisdom and insight into the things of God. The following scriptures point this out:

> **COLOSSIANS 3:16**
> **16 Let the word of Christ dwell in you richly in all wisdom; teaching and admonishing one another in psalms and hymns and spiritual songs, singing with grace in your hearts to the Lord.**
>
> **PSALM 119:105**
> **105 Thy word is a lamp unto my feet, and a light unto my path.**

It is as we study God's Word diligently that we will be able to "rightly divide" it. To "rightly divide" is to understand or present the Word rightly, making "a straight path" of understanding for others to follow.

It is my sincere desire that with the help of this book, you will be able to study God's Word more effectively and improve the quality of your Bible study time, and that these new skills will assist you in drawing closer to God and knowing Him better.

---

[1] *Pleasure and Profit in Bible Study* (Chicago: Moody Press, n.d.) pp. 51,52.

Chapter 2
Organization

Have a Plan

The fatal flaw in most plans and methods of work is that they are not carried out. We fail to see things accomplished not because they are unworkable, but because they are not worked! A method of study is only a guide to work. Find a method of study that works for you, then stick to it. It is also helpful for you to know how to expand your study if you need to. Know where you can go for more material to look at, such as a library. Discuss your findings with someone, and listen to their response. This can help you avoid foolish and unlearned questions (2 Tim. 2:23). After the plan is made, the work remains to be done.

The difficulty is not the lack of time. It is the lack of coordination in the use of time. If you are failing to plan, then you are planning to fail. Start with a simple plan that works for you and stick with it. Make up your mind to spend some time *every day* studying God's Word. Remember, Bible study is one of the most fruitful resolutions that a Christian can make. It can be the turning point in your life, from barren and unfruitful to rich and rewarding.

This change can only be accomplished through faithful, persevering, daily study of the Bible. This study may not be very interesting at first, but you will soon begin to see that the more time you spend in God's Word, the more you will come to love it and the more it will enrich your life.

Be sure that you set aside a certain allotted time to study. You choose the time. Do not allow other things to interrupt your study time. If you cannot give more than fifteen minutes a day, then devote that fifteen minutes faithfully every day. You and the Holy Spirit can accomplish a lot in fifteen minutes a day if you will apply yourself. Whenever possible, lock yourself in with God alone.

Be realistic here. Sit down and figure out how much time you spend doing other things, like watching TV, reading the newspaper, talking on the phone, going to the mall, or whatever it is that you do during a normal week. Then add up the time that you have used. (Do not forget to add sleeping and eating). Remember, everybody has 24 hours in each day. This breaks down into 1,440 minutes.

Always Keep the Bible As the Center of Your Study

You can (should) use other books as you study, but always remember to keep the Bible as the center of your study. You may find it helpful to use other translations of Scripture in your study of God's Word. They *are* Scripture, and may help to enrich your study time, as one version often explains another. This is particularly helpful when you are having difficulty understanding a verse or passage.

Make up Your Mind To *Study* God's Word

A casual reading will not do. So many Christians skim over their Bibles haphazardly, thinking that they are studying God's Word, and then they wonder why their "study time" is not producing any changes in their lives. It is the truths contained in God's Word, once they take hold in our hearts, that bring change in our lives. We must seek out those truths, spend time reading and pondering and meditating on them.

We must consider their impact on our lives, and prayerfully humble ourselves to change our lives when we need to in light of new revelation received.

This, friends, is true study. When you read a verse or passage, ask yourself, *What does this mean to me? How does this affect MY life?* Never allow anyone else, such as your pastor, to do your studying for you. Always insist on doing it for yourself.

> **HEBREWS 4:12,13 (*Moffatt*)**
> **For the Logos of God is a living thing, active and more cutting than any sword with double edge, penetrating to the very division of soul and spirit, joints and marrow — scrutinizing the very thoughts and conceptions of the heart. And no created thing is hidden from Him; all things lie open and exposed before the eyes of Him with whom we have to reckon.**

Be Systematic About Your Study

Do not just take up subjects at random. Think about what you would like to study and make a list. Then go down your list and take up the topics, one by one, and begin a thorough study. This will help you to avoid studying the same topics over and over.

Make Prayer an Important Part of Study Preparation

As you prepare to study you need to ask the Lord to reveal to you what He has for you for today. Every time you open your Bible, ask God to open your spiritual eyes for discernment. If you ask expecting, He will reveal Himself to you through His Word every time.

> **JOHN 16:13,14**
> **13 Howbeit when he, the Spirit of truth, is come, he will guide you into all truth: for he shall not speak**

of himself; but whatsoever he shall hear, that shall
he speak: and he will shew you things to come.
14 He shall glorify me: for he shall receive of mine,
and shall shew it unto you.

The Ephesian and Colossian prayers are excellent to pray
for yourself before you study. I have put these into the first
person to make them easier to use.

EPHESIANS 1:17-23
17 That the God of our Lord Jesus Christ, the
Father of glory, may give unto . . . [me] the spirit of
wisdom and revelation in the knowledge of . . .
[You]:
18 The eyes of . . . [my] understanding are being
enlightened; that . . . [I] may know what is the hope
of his calling, and what the riches of the glory of
his inheritance in the saints,
19 And what is the exceeding greatness of his
power to . . . [me] who believe, according to the
working of his mighty power,
20 Which . . . [You] wrought in Christ, when . . . [You]
raised him from the dead, and set him at . . . [Your]
own right hand in the heavenly places,
21 Far above all principality, and power, and
might, and dominion, and every name that is
named, not only in this world, but also in that
which is to come:
22 And have put all things under his feet, and
gave him to be the head over all things to the
church,
23 Which is his body, the fulness of him that filleth
all in all.

EPHESIANS 3:16-21
16 That . . . [You] would grant . . . [me], according to
the riches of . . . [Your] glory, to be strengthened
with might by . . . [Your] Spirit in . . . [my] inner man;
17 That Christ may dwell in . . . [my] heart by faith;
that . . . [I] being rooted and grounded in love,
18 May be able to comprehend with all saints
what is the breadth, and length, and depth, and
height;

19 And to know the love of Christ, which passeth knowledge, that . . . [I] might be filled with all the fulness of God.
20 Now unto him that is able to do exceeding abundantly above all that . . . [I] ask or think, according to the power that works in . . . [me],
21 Unto him be glory in the church by Christ Jesus throughout all ages, world without end. Amen.

COLOSSIANS 1:9-14
9   For this cause . . . [I] also , since the day . . . [I] heard . . . [the Gospel], do not cease to pray . . . and to desire that . . . [I] might be filled with the knowledge of . . . [Your] will in all wisdom and spiritual understanding;
10 That . . . [I] might walk worthy of the Lord unto all pleasing, being fruitful in every good work, and increasing in the knowledge of God;
11 Strengthened with all might, according to . . . [Your] glorious power, unto all patience and long-suffering with joyfulness;
12 Giving thanks unto the Father, which has made . . . [me able] to be partakers of the inheritance of the saints in light:
13 Who hath delivered . . . [me] from the power of darkness, and hath translated . . . [me] into the kingdom of his dear Son [the Son of Love]:
14 In whom . . . [I] have redemption through his blood, even the remission of sins.

E. W. Kenyon said that too many people treat the Word of God as if it were a common book.[1] Let us remember not to make this mistake.

---

[1] *New Creation Realities,* 12th ed., printed in USA: copyright © 1945,1964 by Kenyon's Gospel Publishing Society), Ch. 2.

Chapter 3
Techniques and Tips For Personal Bible Study

Using Colored Markers

Usually when I look at someone else's Bible that has been marked up and underlined with colored markers, I find that it looks much like several of my own, with no rhyme or reason to the colors that are used. Here are a few tips that I believe will help you put these colored markers to good use.

Always start with a Bible that has no underlining or highlighting in it. Pick out some Greek or Hebrew words that you would like to see in context regardless of how they have been translated into English. For instance, I have used two words for power, *dunamis* and *exousia*. All of the places that *dunamis* was found I underlined in purple and all of the occasions of the listings of *exousia* I underlined in blue. Now by just reading through my Bible I can know instantly which Greek word was used, and without the clutter of Strong's numbers.

Bibles that use the Strong's numbering system are fine enough in their own setting, but for reading without having to get out all your Greek study aids I recommend this method. As I have done this with other words as well, allow me to give you some sort of focal point at which to begin. Remember that this is *your* study and you can choose any words that you would like to use. Plan this out before you begin. Decide how many colors of markers that you plan to use. You will only be able to use one color per Greek or Hebrew word.

Next, make a map of the colors to be used and glue it on the inside cover of your Bible, either front or back. Write out the Greek or Hebrew word with a brief definition of that word. For instance, for the words *logos* and *rhema* you would put "word" for the definition. Be sure to underline your Greek or Hebrew word. You will be surprised at how this will help you to understand what you are reading. Never assume that a word means what it says in the English. For instance, in *Bullinger's Critical Lexicon to the English and Greek New Testament*, we find fourteen different Greek words that are translated into the English word *of*.

Here is a brief list of words that you may want to consider using.

Dunamis = power

Exousia = power

Logos = word

Rhema = word

Sozo = save, heal

Roman Road Approach

Most of us are familiar with the Roman Road method of marking our Bibles or Testaments. The Roman Road is used for leading someone to salvation, but this same method can be used as a sort of chain reference for other topics. You remember that somewhere at the front of your Bible or Testament you write down something like, "Go to Romans 3:23." Then when you turn to Romans 3:23 you make a circle or some sort of distinct marking there that you can locate quickly.

Now, somewhere on this page you will want to say something like, "Go to Romans 5:12." After turning there you will repeat what you have already done on the previous page, except you will want to indicate that you will be going to Romans 6:23. Now you will repeat again this same process with the next few verses, Romans 5:8, Romans 10:9,10, and finally, Romans 10:13. Now you see why this is called the Roman Road.

This approach can be used with any subject that you may wish to study. We will list a few to help you get started, but keep in mind that it will be hard, not to mention messy, to try to insert a verse or verses after you already have them listed. You may want to use an older or inexpensive Bible to begin with. Another hint here for those who are just learning their way around their Bible, or for those studies which happen to fall in the minor prophets, is to write the page number down along with the chapter and verse.

Here are three examples of topics that can be used with this approach:

1. Faith

Matthew 8:13; Matthew 9:28,29; Mark 9:23; Mark 11:22-24; John 11:40; John 15:7; Acts 27:25; Romans 10:17; Romans 12:3; 2 Corinthians 4:18; 2 Corinthians 5:7; Ephesians 6:16; Hebrews 11:1; Hebrews 11:6; Hebrews 11:11; 1 John 5:4.

2. Healing

Exodus 15:26; Exodus 23:25; Deuteronomy 7:15; Psalm 30:2; Psalm 42:11; Psalm 103:2,3; Psalm 105:37; Psalm 107:20; Proverbs 12:18; Proverbs 17:22; Isaiah 53:4,5; Malachi 4:2; Matthew 8:2,3; Matthew 8:16,17, Matthew 9:35; Matthew 14:14; Mark 5:25-34; Acts 3:16; Acts 5:16; Acts 10:38; 1 Peter 2:24; 3 John 2.

3. Finances

Deuteronomy 8:18; 1 Chronicles 29:12; Psalm 23:1; Psalm 34:9,10; Psalm 35:27; Psalm 112:2,3; Proverbs 3:9,10;

Proverbs 8:20,21; Proverbs 22:4; Isaiah 1:19; Malachi 3:10; Luke 6:38; 2 Corinthians 8:9; Philippians 4:19; 1 Timothy 4:8.

Reading Through Proverbs and Psalms

You can read through the Book of Proverbs each month using this easy method. You begin by reading the Proverb that corresponds with the day of the month. For instance, if it is the fifteenth, then read Proverbs 15. Since there are thirty-one chapters in Proverbs, each chapter can correspond to that day of the month. This way you will read the entire Book of Proverbs through in one month, or through twelve times in a year. A good thing about this method is that you can begin anytime.

You may also wish to include the Book of Psalms with this reading. The way that you do this is by starting with the day of the month once again and read there. Let's use the fifteenth again. You will read Psalm 15, then, since there are 150 Psalms, you need to read four more Psalms each day to completely read Psalms through in a single month. So the best thing to do is to add thirty to each Psalm that you read. For instance, beginning with Psalm 15, add thirty and turn to Psalm 45. After reading this Psalm, add another thirty and read Psalm 75. Next we will add thirty and read Psalm 105, and finally add the last thirty and read Psalm 135.

This is a good approach because it is easy to know which Psalms to read, and since the Book of Psalms is actually five separate books combined into one, you will be reading a Psalm from each of the five separate books each day.

When Should I Study the Bible?

One of the most frequently asked questions about Bible study is, *When is the best time to study?* The Scriptures encourage us to seek God early. This could have a double meaning, that is, early in our day or early in our situation.

Early in some people's day may not be what others think of as early. Do not let someone else's schedule be what determines yours. Set your own schedule, then follow it. Then, as we mentioned, if you allow the Holy Spirit to direct your study time, you will be seeking the Lord early in your situation.

> **PSALM 63:1**
> 1   O God, thou art my God; early will I seek thee: my soul thirsteth for thee, my flesh longeth for thee in a dry and thirsty land, where no water is.

> **ISAIAH 26:9**
> 9   With my soul have I desired thee in the night; yea, with my spirit within me will I seek thee early: for when thy judgments are in the earth, the inhabitants of the world will learn righteousness.

Remember that a daily study of God's Word is necessary for spiritual growth. Until we learn to feed on the Word of God for ourselves, we will only be getting God's Word secondhand. We must search the Scriptures for ourselves on a daily basis.

> **ACTS 17:11**
> 11 These were more noble than those in Thessalonica, in that they received the word with all readiness of mind, and searched the scriptures daily, whether those things were so.

Chapter 4

How Should I Study the Bible?

Remember To Pray First

Always pray before you read your Bible. The single most important aid to Bible study is prayer. Clear your mind of all thoughts that are weighing on you and ask the Holy Spirit to speak to your heart as you study. Ask the Lord to open the eyes of your spiritual understanding and give you revelation needed for daily living.

> **LUKE 24:45**
> **45 Then opened he their understanding, that they might understand the scriptures.**
>
> **PSALM 119:18**
> **18 Open thou mine eyes, that I may behold wondrous things out of thy law.**

Prayer will help you to keep what you read in proper perspective. Then, after you have asked the Lord for revelation and insight, it is important to thank Him for it. James 1:5 says that if anyone lacks wisdom, he should ask the Father and it will be given him if he asks in faith.

Keep a Right Attitude

As you prepare to study God's Word, remember to approach your Bible study with a humble heart and willing attitude. Jesus said: ". . . *I thank thee, O Father, Lord of heaven and earth, because thou hast hid these things from the wise and prudent, and hast revealed them unto babes"* (Matt. 11:25). We must study God's Word with a humble heart and will totally surrendered to Him, for it is only then that we will receive revelation.

Do not study the Bible to find a verse to corroborate your own view or ideas. Rather study it to find out what it really says. If you look hard enough, you can find Scripture that can be twisted to mean anything. Be careful when looking for scriptures to prove something. Make sure you keep your mind and your heart open to the Holy Spirit.

Allow God's Word To Speak to You Personally

Study the Word of God as if it were God speaking to you personally, because it is. Have you ever wished that God would come down and speak to you face to face, like He talked with Abraham? Well, we have something better than Abraham had. Only on rare occasions did God speak to Abraham, but God speaks to our hearts every time we open our Bibles. Allowing God's Word to speak to us personally each time we read it will make the Bible come alive.

Romans 8:16 tells us that the Spirit bears witness with our spirits that we are the sons of God. This means the Lord is speaking to us twenty-four hours a day. We can learn to flow with the Spirit — to listen to Him explain the Word of God to our spirits.

Practice What You Learn

Finally, you must put into practice what you have learned. James says, *"But be ye doers of the word, and not hearers only, deceiving your own selves"* (James 1:22). We are only deceiving ourselves if we read and study God's Word but do not practice it. Study God's Word to find out how to live pleasing to God, and then live that way!

We must keep in mind that reading the Bible and studying the Bible are not the same thing. Reading is not studying, but reading is very important and helpful. Occasionally we need to read through a book or portion as though we were taking a drive in the country, relaxing and enjoying the scenery — not stopping to investigate anything in particular, but just reading for pure enjoyment. Reading the Bible will do things for your spiritual life that study cannot do.

You may want to find a good *read-through-the-Bible* list, or perhaps just check off the books/chapters as you read them. Either way, a systematic reading of the Bible will give you a good overall picture of God's Word.

Study the Bible Itself

Too often people make the mistake of studying about the Bible and not really studying the Bible at all. They may use some fine word study books, and look through some good commentaries. But that is not studying the Word of God. One must actually feed upon the Word of God itself to gain the nourishment needed for spiritual growth.

ACTS 17:11
11 These were more noble than those in Thessalonica, in that they received the word with all readiness of mind, and searched the scriptures daily, whether those things were so.

MARK 7:13
13 Making the word of God of none effect through your tradition, which ye have delivered: and many such like things do ye.

Examine the Scriptures

With so many people trying to explain to us what the Word of God says, it is best to take the time to find out for ourselves just what it does say. Too many people rely upon their pastor or some television minister for their spiritual nourishment. I could eat at the best restaurant in town and then tell you how good the food is there, but if you do not go there for yourself, you will never know how good the food really is. What your pastor tells you is only secondhand information until you get in and examine for yourself what the Word of God says.

> **MATTHEW 13:23**
> **23 But he that received seed into the good ground is he that heareth the word, and understandeth it; which also beareth fruit, and bringeth forth, some an hundredfold, some sixty, some thirty.**

> **JEREMIAH 15:16**
> **16 Thy words were found, and I did eat them; and thy word was unto me the joy and rejoicing of mine heart: for I am called by thy name, O Lord God of hosts.**

Store the Word in Your Heart

Your heart, like any other storehouse, can hold a huge amount of God's Word. But do not think that just because it was full last week that you can still draw from its resources like you did then. You have to replenish the Word that you store up in your heart. Learn to meditate the Word of God, that is to speak it over and over to yourself, turning it over in your mind and dwelling upon what it says.

> **PSALM 119:11**
> **11 Thy word have I hid in mine heart, that I might not sin against thee.**

JOHN 14:23
23 Jesus answered and said unto him, If a man love me, he will keep my words: and my Father will love him, and we will come unto him, and make our abode with him.

PSALM 1:2
2   But his delight is in the law of the Lord; and in his law doth he meditate day and night.

PSALM 40:8
8   I delight to do thy will, O my God: yea, thy law is within my heart.

Study the Whole Bible

When Jesus explained to His disciples Who He was, He used the whole Word of God. A great deal of false teaching would be done away with if we would look at certain teachings from the whole Counsel of God.

LUKE 24:27
27 And beginning at Moses and all the prophets, he expounded unto them in all the scriptures the things concerning himself.

Study More Than Favorite Subjects

We sometimes have certain subjects that we like to study, and may even specialize in them. They may be very good topics that we choose to study, such as healing, prophecy, judgment, and so forth. But by spending all of our time on these topics, we will neglect other areas that are just as important for a balanced spiritual life. In order for our bodies to get all the nutrition they need, we need to eat more than just our favorite kind of food.

In the same way, we need to not be so selective with what we study from God's Word. Just as there must be a balance to our eating habits, there must also be a balance to our study habits. This does not mean that we cannot focus on a particular subject for study, but we must also remember to take the rest of the Bible into account. You may be surprised to see how often a particular subject will show up in an area where you least expect it.

Study the Bible As the Word of God

The Bible is not just some good book that teaches us how to live; it is alive. It is alive with the very life of God residing in it. In it are all the answers to your problems. It is your operator's handbook for daily living. Do not think of the Bible as just an ancient book. It is alive and powerful. It is powerful enough to separate soul and spirit, and to know the thoughts and intents of the heart.

> **1 THESSALONIANS 2:13**
> **13 For this cause also thank we God without ceasing, because, when ye received the word of God which ye heard of us, ye received it not as the word of men, but as it is in truth, the word of God, which effectually worketh also in you that believe.**

> **HEBREWS 4:12**
> **12 For the word of God is quick, and powerful, and sharper than any twoedged sword, piercing even to the dividing asunder of soul and spirit, and of the joints and marrow, and is discerner of the thoughts and intents of the heart.**

Read From Various Translations

Reading the Bible from various translations can give you a fresh perspective on familiar Scripture passages. There are several good translations now in print as well as many out-of-print versions which are still readily available. We will look at Bible translations in more depth later.

When reading a book or passage through in several translations, it is often best to begin with the version you usually use for your personal study and reading. I recommend that, besides your regular study Bible, you keep a clean, unmarked Bible, without notes or comments, so that you can read without distractions. Read the passage or book through in this version first. Then read the passage again the next time in another version.

You may want to continue this for several days using various translations, then go back and read it again in your usual version. You will be surprised at the new insight this will bring to the passage you have been reading.

Make Outlines

Making an outline is an excellent way to study a book or topic. You may want to begin by using someone else's outline, changing it and adding to it to make it your own.

When making an outline, you may wish to use your word study books and other study tools or anything that will help you most. If you are not very knowledgeable about outline formats, do not worry about it. Remember that you are not being graded on your English. This is your study, and most likely you will be the only one using it.

Learn To Use Study Tools

Another great help to Bible study is the use of Bible study tools, such as concordances, lexicons, and Bible dictionaries. Some of these might include *Strong's Exhaustive Concordance of the Bible*, *Young's Analytical Concordance to the Bible*, *Thayer's Greek-English Lexicon of the New Testament*, and

Vine's Expository Dictionary of Biblical Words. These are just a few of the many volumes in print that you can utilize in your study time. But remember that just owning the books will not help you. You must find the ones that will be the most helpful to *you*. Never get a study tool just because your pastor or Bible teacher has it. Make sure that you get something that you will use.

Chapter 5
Methods of Study

1) The Synthetic Method

The Synthetic Method of Bible study is a method by which we can see the overall picture of a book or subject. Do not confuse the word "synthetic" as used here with its more common definition, that is, something manmade. In the context of Bible study, it has more of the meaning of seeing the Bible from a bird's eye view. The word "synthetic" is borrowed from the Greek. It takes the preposition *syn*, which means "together," and the verbal root *the*, which means "to put," so that we come up with the meaning *a putting, or placing together*.

To do a synthetic study, start by reading a book or passage through several times. Look for the main theme of the book or passage first. Some examples would be:

- *The Book of Colossians speaks of Christ and the Church.*
- *The Book of Ephesians speaks of the believer and the Church.*
- *The Book of Galatians speaks of the believers' freedom found in Christ.*

The synthetic method pays no attention to details, rather it looks at the book or passage as a whole. While doing a synthetic approach to study, look for distinct themes that run through the book or passage. Watch how these themes develop. Is there any one verse or passage that states this theme more

clearly than any other? There are many possible ways of finding clues, so look for any statements which the author may give
concerning the content of the book.

An example of such a statement would be in First
Corinthians, where we find such statements as *now concerning*.

> 1 CORINTHIANS 7:1
> 1   NOW CONCERNING the things whereof ye
> wrote unto me: It is good for a man not to touch a
> woman.
>
> 1 CORINTHIANS 7:25
> 25 NOW CONCERNING virgins I have no com-
> mandment of the Lord: yet I give my judgment, as
> one that hath obtained mercy of the Lord to be
> faithful.
>
> 1 CORINTHIANS 12:1
> 1   NOW CONCERNING spiritual gifts, brethren, I
> would not have you ignorant.
>
> 1 CORINTHIANS 16:1
> 1   NOW CONCERNING the collection for the
> saints, as I have given order to the churches of
> Galatia, even so do ye.

Another example would be in Matthew's Gospel, where we
find such statements as *when Jesus had finished*.

> MATTHEW 11:1 (*RSV*)
> And WHEN JESUS HAD FINISHED instructing his
> twelve disciples, he went on from there to teach
> and preach in their cities.
>
> MATTHEW 13:53 (*RSV*)
> And WHEN JESUS HAD FINISHED these parables,
> he went away from there.
>
> MATTHEW 19:1 (*RSV*)
> Now WHEN JESUS HAD FINISHED these sayings,
> he went away from Galilee and entered the region
> of Judea beyond the Jordan.

MATTHEW 26:1 *(RSV)*
WHEN JESUS HAD FINISHED all these sayings,
he said to his disciples.

Yet another example is seen in Hebrews where we find the
phrase *let us*, which sometimes appears to complete a section
of teaching.

HEBREWS 4:1
1   LET US therefore fear, lest, a promise being left
us of entering into his rest, any of you should seem
to come short of it.

HEBREWS 4:11
11 LET US labour therefore to enter into that rest,
lest any man fall after the same example of unbelief.

HEBREWS 4:14
14 Seeing then that we have a great high priest,
that is passed into the heavens, Jesus the Son of
God, LET US hold fast our profession.

HEBREWS 4:16
16 LET US therefore come boldly unto the throne
of grace, that we may obtain mercy, and find grace
to help in time of need.

HEBREWS 6:1
1   Therefore leaving the principles of the doctrine of Christ, LET US go on unto perfection; not
laying again the foundation of repentance from
dead works, and of faith toward God.

HEBREWS 10:22
22 LET US draw near with a true heart in full
assurance of faith, having our hearts sprinkled
from an evil conscience, and our bodies washed
with pure water.

HEBREWS 10:23
23 LET US hold fast the profession of our faith
without wavering; (for he is faithful that promised).

HEBREWS 10:24
24 And LET US consider one another to provoke unto love and to good works.

HEBREWS 12:1
Wherefore seeing we also are compassed about with so great a cloud of witnesses, LET US lay aside every weight, and the sin which doth so easily beset us, and LET US run with patience the race that is set before us.

HEBREWS 12:28
28 Wherefore we receiving a kingdom which cannot be moved, LET US have grace, whereby we may serve God acceptably with reverence and godly fear.

HEBREWS 13:13
13 LET US go forth therefore unto him without the camp, bearing his reproach.

HEBREWS 13:15
15 By him therefore LET US offer the sacrifice of praise to God continually, that is, the fruit of our lips giving thanks to his name.

Statements like these are not always conclusive to the view of the book, they are only a good place to start looking. You may want to use several different translations in this study. Look at the difference when we use *The Revised Standard Version* in First Corinthians for the phrase *now concerning*.

1 CORINTHIANS 7:1 (*RSV*)
NOW CONCERNING the matters about which you wrote. It is well for a man not to touch a woman.

1 CORINTHIANS 7:25 (*RSV*)
NOW CONCERNING the unmarried, I have no command of the Lord, but I give my opinion as one who by the Lord's mercy is trustworthy.

1 CORINTHIANS 8:1 (*RSV*)
NOW CONCERNING food offered to idols: we
know that all of us possess knowledge. Knowledge
puffs up, but love builds up.

1 CORINTHIANS 12:1 (*RSV*)
NOW CONCERNING spiritual gifts, brethren, I do
not want you to be uninformed.

1 CORINTHIANS 16:1 (*RSV*)
NOW CONCERNING the contribution for the
saints: as I directed the churches of Galatia, so you
also are to do.

When looking at themes, also look for sudden changes of
subject matter, or a sudden change in persons being spoken of.
Pay attention to changes in language form, or a shifting in
narration. A good way to see these changes is to follow the text
by paragraph. Start looking at each paragraph as a unit, then
place the paragraphs together that maintain the same
thought. Paragraphs, of course, are not in the original text, but
will provide a sound study, normally. An example of where this
is not true can be found in Galatians 5:1. This verse belongs to
the passage that was left behind in chapter 4. Chapter 5
should have been started with verse 2.

It is also helpful to find and read as many outlines as you
can on the book that you are studying. Outlines may be found
in many study Bibles. Outlines may also be found in many
commentaries and reference books. As you begin to see a certain form of development taking place, then begin with your
own outline. As you look over these outlines from varied
sources you will notice that some of the major points of the
outlines are the same, but that there are differences in the
body of the outline.

You need not concern yourself with how good your outline
is, only that it is helping you to gain more understanding of
the passage or book that you are studying. And, of course, you

can use an outline already made as the basis of your outline. If you do this I would suggest that you use two or more outlines to work from. This will give you a more well-rounded view of the subject or book you are outlining.

2) The Devotional Method

The devotional method may be used alone in studying or in conjunction with other study methods. You can use it to study a whole book, although this takes time, or you can use it on selected passages or even just a single verse. The term "method" may be misleading here since it is not a mechanical method like the others. Rather it is one by which you actually feed your spirit man. This method is not a learned technique. It should be done out of your spirit. You must earnestly wish to seek the mind of God. You must maintain a spirit of humility as you listen to the voice of God. You must enter into a place of worship to experience the Presence of God.

Remember that there can be no set of rules that are written in stone. You will discover that you will get out of each text as much as you are willing to give it. You can also benefit from the use of devotional type books by various authors. Many of these books have, over a period of time, come to be used as daily devotional books by many. Some good examples would be: *The Daily Study Bible*, by William Barclay; *Matthew Henry's Commentary on the Whole Bible*; or the writings of John G. Lake, E. W. Kenyon, and Smith Wigglesworth.

In the late 1700s, a man by the name of Philip Doddridge did a paraphrase of the New Testament which he called *The Family Expositor*. It was his intention that it be used for family devotions, when the family would sit down together and spend time around the Word of God. This New Testament, unfortunately, is hard to find today, but the need for family devotions still exists.

It was because of this need that Kenneth Taylor paraphrased what we call today *The Living Bible*. He would paraphrase sections of the New Testament letters for his children while commuting on a train to and from work. Someone happened to see these bits of paraphrases and encouraged him to print them.

If you do not feel like you are able or qualified to paraphrase Scripture for your family, then pick up some easy-to-understand Bibles. Whether they are translations or paraphrases is up to you and your preference. The important thing is that you use them. This is a very important part of your study life, for how can you explain something to your children or spouse if you do not understand it yourself?

Realize that understanding will come from this method just by practicing it. I have a copy of a paraphrase of certain books of the New Testament that a lady did just for herself and her children, and I believe that it is one of the best that I have ever read. She made it by pouring over other translations and writing down what the Holy Spirit gave her concerning the verses that she read. What I want you to see is that you can do this as well.

I have done some paraphrasing like this and have found that this is one of the best ways to know what the Word of God says. You must have an idea of what is being said in order to paraphrase it; therefore, you need to have studied the Word of God. You may have heard your pastor or someone while they were preaching say something like "this verse means such and such." You may have even said that yourself to someone else. This is what it means to paraphrase.

Proper Preparation and Proper Discipline

First spend some time in prayer, clearing your mind of distracting thoughts. This will help you to center your thoughts upon things of the Lord as well as things of the Spirit. This method is actually more of a spiritual exercise. While the other methods are for gathering the food to eat, this method is the actual eating of the food. Recognize that at times your mind will wander, but that this generally lessens after a season.

Questions you should ask as you read are: What does this passage show me about Jesus? How can I apply it to my life? Does some experience that I may have had line up with what I am reading? Is there some truth that must be incorporated into my daily life? Does any new revelation line up with the rest of God's Word? These and other questions, along with thoroughly reading, pondering, and meditating on what you have read, will help to solidify God's Word in your heart and life.

3) The Biographical Method

The biographical method is simply studying the history of a person who is mentioned in the Bible. It includes all events recorded in their life. It also includes any text that may give us some clue as to who they were. There are nearly 3,000 people mentioned in the Bible. Do not confuse certain ones who happen to have the same name. A good example of this can be seen using the name of Noah. There are two different people in the Bible by the name of Noah. The first we all know as the one whom God called to build an ark. But the second person we find named Noah is a different person, and a woman!

NUMBERS 26:33
33 And Zelophehad the son of Hepher had no sons, but daughters: and the names of the daughters of Zelophehad were Mahlah, and Noah, Hoglah, Milcah, and Tirzah.

NUMBERS 27:1
1   Then came the daughters of Zelophehad, the son of Hepher, the son of Gilead, the son of Machir, the son of Manasseh, of the families of Manasseh

the son of Joseph: and these are the names of his daughters; Mahlah, Noah, and Hoglah, and Milcah, and Tirzah.

NUMBERS 36:11
11 For Mahlah, Tirzah, and Hoglah, and Milcah, and Noah, the daughters of Zelophehad, were married unto their father's brothers' sons.

JOSHUA 17:3
3 But Zelophehad, the son of Hepher, the son of Gilead, the son of Machir, the son of Manasseh, had no sons, but daughters: and these are the names of his daughters, Mahlah, and Noah, Hoglah, Milcah, and Tirzah.

A quick look at these passages and we are easily convinced that this is indeed a different Noah. But not all names are that easy. For example, look at Gaius.

ACTS 19:29
29 And the whole city was filled with confusion: and having caught Gaius and Aristarchus, men of Macedonia, Paul's companions in travel, they rushed with one accord into the theater.

ACTS 20:4
4 And there accompanied him into Asia Sopater of Berea; and of the Thessalonians, Aristarchus and Secundus; and Gaius of Derbe, and Timotheus; and of Asia, Tychicus and Trophimus.

ROMANS 16:23
23 Gaius mine host, and of the whole church, saluteth you. Erastus the chamberlain of the city saluteth you, and Quartus a brother.

1 CORINTHIANS 1:14
14 I thank God that I baptized none of you, but Crispus and Gaius.

3 JOHN 1
1   The elder unto the wellbeloved Gaius, whom I
love in the truth.

Is this the same person or not? No one really knows. And since it is not our intention to prove either way, but rather to show you the method of this type of study, we will leave that bit of research up to you.

There are five Marys, five Johns, five Jameses, and more than twenty Nathans. You can benefit from studying certain lives. The lives of Bible characters are examples to us, good or bad. Some good examples are Paul, David, and Moses. Some bad examples are Ananias and Sapphira, Demas and Balaam. We can be inspired by the good examples of faith, and we can study the people in the light of their historical significance.

The type of questions you could ask are: Who was this person? What made this person important? What did this person do with his life? What were the particular qualities of his character? What role did this person play in God's overall plan? Was this role positive or negative? What can be learned from observing this person's life and example?

4) Analytical Method

The analytical method consists of pulling apart sections of Scripture, words or phrases, then analyzing them in detail. This method involves the use of study tools, some of which are discussed in this book, such as *Strong's Exhaustive Concordance of the Bible*, *Vine's Expository Dictionary of Biblical Words*, and various Bible dictionaries, handbooks, and so forth.

This method generally involves the study of words, and sometimes phrases, in whole or in part. It may also involve noting the occurrences of words, and often deals with word meanings.

As an example, I have listed the first verse in Psalm 91, using word studies from titles that are discussed in this book as well as a few others in order to round out the study and give a clearer understanding of what you can do. I have also included some notes from a few commentaries and Bible translations. This can be one of the most rewarding methods of studying you can use since you are able to examine extensively the verse or passage you are studying.

I suggest that you keep your work neat so that you can use it over the years. You may also wish to arrange it in a way that you can add to it as you find other references to your subject. For instance, if you work with translations, start each verse on a separate piece of paper. Then when you run across another translation you would like to add, you can easily add it to the end of the list. The same is true with commentaries and quotes from various writers. Since this is your study, you can use as much or as little material as you want to. Never let anyone tell you that you use too much of one thing or not enough of another. Allow yourself to grow into your work. Let it develop naturally.

What I have provided is only an example. If possible, find some other examples to compare, and use what helps you. This is the main crux of this type of studying to help you grow in the things of God.

The numbers used in the following word study example are from *Strong's Exhaustive Concordance of the Bible*.

PSALM 91:1
1   He that DWELLETH in the SECRET PLACE of the MOST HIGH shall ABIDE under the SHADOW of the ALMIGHTY.

DWELLETH (#3427)

Strong's Concordance: . . .*by implic.* [implication] to *dwell, to remain; causat.* [causative] *to settle, to marry.* . . .

Gesenius: (1) . . . *a sitting down, habitations, places . . . a throne, a bed.*

Wilson: *to sit down, to seat oneself; to remain, abide, tarry; to dwell, to dwell in, to inhabit; to dwell (together), as a family, in concord.*

Vine's: *to dwell, sit, abide, inhabit, remain.*

(Note: All references to Vine's are taken from *Vine's Expository Dictionary of Biblical Words*).

SECRET (#5643) PLACE

Strong's Concordance: . . . *a cover . . .*

Gesenius: *(3) protection, defense . . .*

Theological Wordbook of the Old Testament: Hiding Place . . . (God) himself is ever a place of refuge and protection from all dangers for the believer . . .

MOST HIGH (#5945)

Strong's Concordance: . . . *an elevation, i.e. (adj.) [adjective] lofty (compar.)* (compare); *as title, the Supreme. . . .*

ABIDE (#3885)

Strong's Concordance: . . . *by impl.* [implication] *to stay permanently . . .*

Gesenius: *(2) . . To shew oneself stubborn . . .*

Wilson: . . . *to lodge, to stay all night; to continue in a settled state.*

Theological Wordbook of the Old Testament: . . . *The theological usage emphasizes the brevity of God's anger as opposed to the life-giving power of his abundant favor. . . The best verse of all is Ps. 91:1.*

SHADOW (#6738)

Wilson: *3c shade; also as affording shelter, protection.*

Theological Wordbook of the Old Testament: In a positive sense, "shadow" conveys the ideas of shade, protection, and defense . . . Yahweh is the shade of the source of protection for his people (Ps. 121:5f.; Isa. 25:4). Therefore the Psalmist prays that God may hide him under "the shadow of his wings" (Ps. 17:8; cf. 36:7; 91:1). . . .

ALMIGHTY (#7706)

Gesenius: . . . *most powerful, Almighty. . .*

Pick: . . . *the all-sufficient One.*

Commentary Comparisons

Benson:

He that makes God his habitation and refuge, as he is called in verse 9, that has recourse to him, and relies on him in his dangers and difficulties; that has access to him, intercourse with him, and worships within the veil, living a life of constant communion with him; shall abide under the shadow of the Almighty; He shall not be disappointed of his hope, but shall find a quiet and safe resting-place under the divine care . . . It is justly observed here by Dr. Horne, that "in all dangers, whether spiritual or corporal, the members of Christ's mystical body may reflect, with comfort, that they are under the same almighty Protector."

Cohen:

. . . *shadow: The image is of a mother-bird sheltering her young beneath her wings (cf. v.4), and hide me in the shadow of thy wings, 17:8.*

. . . *Almighty: This appellation like Most High, indicates God's power to provide the refuge.*

Callan:

Hebrew: Shelter, or hiding place, that is, the bosom of God. The just man reposes on the bosom of God, like an infant in its mother arms.

Translation Comparisons

PSALM 91:1
1   He that dwelleth in the secret place of the most High shall abide under the shadow of the Almighty.

PSALM 91:1 (*Lesser*)
He who sitteth under the protection of the Most High, shall rest under the shadow of the Almighty.

PSALM 91:1 (*Fanchiotti*)
He who lives in the secret hiding-places of the Most High God will be safe in the care of the Almighty.

PSALM 91:1 (*The Book of Common Prayer*)
Whoso dwelleth under the defense of the Most High, shall abide under the shadow of the Almighty.

PSALM 91:1(*Harrison*)
He who lives as a ward of the Most High shall repose under the protection of the Almighty.

PSALM 91:1 (*Fillion*)
He that dwelleth in the aid of the most High, shall abide under the protection of the God of Jacob.

PSALM 91:1 (*Brandt*)
That one whose faith is focused on God, who finds his security in Him.

PSALM 91:1 (*Noli*)
All of us who dwell under his shelter are protected by Almighty God.

PSALM 91:1 (*Edington*)
**Anyone who loves the Lord is able to live in the
shadow of God's majesty.**

5) Topical Method

The Topical Method is a method in which one subject is
selected from any of the many subjects mentioned in the Bible.
It is usually studied with regard to its context. If the subject is
a person, then the study is biographical in nature. First select
a topic in the Bible that you are interested in, then pursue the
occurrences of that subject. The topic may consist of a theme or
concept; it may be a word or a phrase. For example, if you are
studying the topic of healing as a theme you will find many
occurrences that do not contain the word *heal* or *healing*.

MATTHEW 9:22
**22 But Jesus turned him about, and when he saw
her, he said, Daughter, be of good comfort; thy
faith hath made thee whole. And the woman was
made whole from that hour.**

MATTHEW 15:28
**28 Then Jesus answered and said unto her, O
woman, great is thy faith: be it unto thee even as
thou wilt. And her daughter was made whole from
that very hour.**

MARK 6:56
**56 And whithersoever he entered, into villages, or
cities, or country, they laid the sick in the streets,
and besought him that they might touch if it were
but the border of his garment: and as many as
touched him were made whole.**

LUKE 7:50
**50 And he said to the woman, Thy faith hath saved
thee; go in peace.**

LUKE 8:50
50 But when Jesus heard it, he answered him, saying, Fear not: believe only, and she shall be made whole.

LUKE 18:42
42 And Jesus said unto him, Receive thy sight: thy faith hath saved thee.

JOHN 5:4
4 For an angel went down at a certain season into the pool, and troubled the water: whosoever then first after the troubling of the water stepped in was made whole of whatsoever disease he had.

JOHN 5:9
9 And immediately the man was made whole, and took up his bed, and walked: and on the same day was the Sabbath.

JOHN 7:23
23 If a man on the sabbath day receive circumcision, that the law of Moses should not be broken; are ye angry at me, because I have made a man every whit whole on the sabbath day?

You may, however, be looking up a single word that is translated "heal" or "healing" from the Greek or Hebrew language and note all of its occurrences regardless of the way that it is translated in other passages. We can see by using *Thayer's A Greek-English Lexicon of the New Testament* that the Greek word *therapeuo* (ther-ap-yoó-o) (Strong #2323) has been rendered *heal* in the *King James Version* of the Bible thirty-eight times, *cure* five times, and *worship* one time for a total of forty-four times.

It means: 1) to serve, do service; and 2) to heal, cure, restore to health. We would have no way of knowing that in Acts 17:25 the word *worshipped* is the same word that has been translated as *heal* or *cure*.

ACTS 17:25
25 Neither is worshipped with men's hands, as
though he needed any thing, seeing he giveth to all
life, and breath, and all things.

6) Practical Method

All Christians know that the Word of God is their source
for daily guidance and direction for their lives. As such the
Bible brings us into a closer relationship with God the Father,
God the Son, and God the Holy Spirit. By studying the Bible
in a practical way, we see the truths we need to live by today,
as well as a clearer path for tomorrow.

The practical method involves looking at the way the
book/passage applies to you in a practical way. How does this
verse or passage affect my daily life? How can I apply it for
everyday living? How does it apply to my Christian walk?
Entire books or short passages may be studied in this way.
Some good examples for this type of study include the Book
of Proverbs, the Book of James, and the Sermon on the
Mount. This method lends toward personal application.
Sometimes it is corrective. Sometimes it shows us things that
we need to change, or things that we need to incorporate into
our lives.

These six methods show some of the various ways to
approach Bible study. There are many more good methods for
study, some of which you may run across from time to time. You
may find that you will want to incorporate these into your
study time as well. Even though you will have a favorite
method, occasionally utilizing other methods will enhance your
study time. Certain subjects lend themselves more readily to
one method than another. Use the information in this chapter
to help you expand your study time and make this expansion
easier for you.

Chapter 6
Rules of Interpretation

Have you ever noticed how two individuals, both very sincere, can read a passage of Scripture and come up with two totally different interpretations of that passage? How, then, can we know that we are interpreting what we read accurately?

Of course, the first thing one must do before attempting to understand any passage of Scripture is to ask for the Holy Spirit's guidance and insight. Then, there are a few principles, or rules of interpretation, that we must refer to in our study. These rules of interpretation are widely accepted and should be used as general guidelines when attempting to better understand or interpret a Scripture passage.

1) Always Observe the Context

This is the first and perhaps the most important principle of Bible interpretation. Begin by asking yourself, "What is the setting of this book/passage? What is the time frame and under what circumstances did the author write it? Who is speaking? Is God speaking, or is man speaking?"

Example:

> **JOB 1:21**
> **21 And said, Naked came I out of my mother's womb, and naked shall I return thither: the Lord gave, and the Lord hath taken away; blessed be the name of the Lord.**

We see here an example of a true statement, but not the truth. This was Job speaking about what he *thought* had happened.

The second thing you must ask yourself is, "Who is being spoken to?"

Example:

> **1 CORINTHIANS 10:32**
> **32 Give none offence, neither to the Jews, nor to the Gentiles, nor to the church of God.**

We can see from this verse that God sees people in three categories: Jew, Gentile, and Church of God. We need to consider which of these three categories of people God is speaking to.

Likewise, when the Bible speaks of Mount Zion it includes you and me, the Church.

> **HEBREWS 12:22-24**
> **22 But ye are come unto mount Sion, and unto the city of the living God, the heavenly Jerusalem, and to an innumerable company of angels,**
> **23 To the general assembly and church of the firstborn, which are written in heaven, and to God the Judge of all, and to the spirits of just men made perfect,**
> **24 And to Jesus the mediator of the new covenant, and to the blood of sprinkling, that speaketh better things than that of Abel.**

In the Old Testament, when the Bible speaks of Mount Sinai, it is always referring to the Law, or the Jews.

> **GALATIANS 4:24**
> **24 Which things are an allegory: for these are the two covenants; the one from the mount Sinai, which gendereth to bondage, which is Agar.**

2) Learn to Allow the Bible to Interpret Itself

From the following verses, we can be sure that God Himself put the Scriptures together.

> **2 TIMOTHY 3:16**
> **16 All scripture is given by inspiration of God, and is profitable for doctrine, for reproof, for correction, for instruction in righteousness.**

> **1 PETER 1:10-12**
> **10 Of which salvation the prophets have inquired and searched diligently, who prophesied of the grace that should come unto you:**
> **11 Searching what, or what manner of time the Spirit of Christ which was in them did signify, when it testified beforehand the sufferings of Christ, and the glory that should follow.**
> **12 Unto whom it was revealed, that not unto themselves, but unto us they did minister the things, which are now reported unto you by them that have preached the gospel unto you with the Holy Ghost sent down from heaven; which things the angels desire to look into.**

We also know that the Bible speaks to all of us the same.

> **2 PETER 1:20**
> **20 Knowing this first, that no prophecy of the scripture is of any private interpretation.**

Since God is the author of the Bible, we know that it all flows together. This remains true in spite of the fact that Scripture came to us through men of varied backgrounds, and has been translated by many people into many varied forms. God's Word is the best commentary upon itself.

3) Do Not Over Spiritualize Everything

Most passages mean just what they say. Consider the literal meaning first before looking for a hidden meaning.

4) Assert an Unassuming Attitude

Do not be quick to form final or dogmatic conclusions about the meaning of a passage. Reflect on the passage in the light of the rest of the Bible. You must spend time with the Holy Spirit to allow the true meaning of a passage to come to light.

5) Study Parallel Passages

Study the parallel passages of the Bible. (A parallel passage contains the same narrative, events or information as another passage in a different book of the Bible). Ephesians and Colossians are parallel in many passages, as are First and Second Kings and First and Second Chronicles. The synoptic Gospels (Matthew, Mark, and Luke) are a very good place to study parallel passages. Realize that not all passages that appear upon first examination to be parallel always are parallel.

Chapter 7
Building and Using a Library

A good library is one of the most helpful resources a Christian can have. The reason for building a personal study library is, of course, to have the tools you need at hand when you need them. You should, however, start out small, adding a few volumes at a time as you see that you need them and as you can afford them. This way your library will grow over the years and become a source of great assistance to you in your study time.

As your library grows, the range of topics your books cover and the number of different authors will also grow. For example, you may not want any titles on the lives of the prophets or apostles at this time, but later you may find this is something you would like to study. Or, you may find a particular author, such as Andrew Murray, whose teaching you enjoy reading. You may want to pick up more of his books to add to your library in the future. And remember, if a book blesses you now when you read it, it will bless you when you read it again.

Often as you are studying, you will find that the Holy Spirit is leading you in a certain direction. If you have a variety of study tools at hand, you will be able to immediately look up the word, topic, or verse that the Holy Spirit is directing you to and study it. This way, the revelation or leading of God will not "grow cold" as it might if you had to delay your study, for instance, by borrowing or buying the tools you need.

Having your own library of resources to consult will:

1) Prevent you from being taken by the traditions of men.

COLOSSIANS 2:8
8   Beware lest any man spoil you through philos-
ophy and vain deceit, after the tradition of men,
after the rudiments of the world, and not after
Christ.

2) Help to keep us from listening to seducing spirits.

1 TIMOTHY 4:1,2
1   Now the Spirit speaketh expressly, that in the
latter times some shall depart from the faith,
giving heed to seducing spirits, and doctrines of
devils;
2   Speaking lies in hypocrisy; having their conscience seared with a hot iron.

3) Help to keep you on track when false doctrine is taught.

1 TIMOTHY 6:3-5
3   If any man teach otherwise, and consent not to
wholesome words, even the words of our Lord
Jesus Christ, and to the doctrine which is according to godliness;
4   He is proud, knowing nothing, but doting about
questions and strifes of words, whereof cometh
envy, strife, railings, evil surmisings,
5   Perverse disputings of men of corrupt minds,
and destitute of the truth, supposing that gain is
godliness: from such withdraw thyself.

4) Help to keep you from being deceived.

2 TIMOTHY 3:13
13 But evil men and seducers shall wax worse and
worse, deceiving, and being deceived.

5) Cause your heart to be established with grace.

HEBREWS 13:9
9   Be not carried about with divers and strange
doctrines. For it is a good thing that the heart be

**established with grace; not with meats, which have
not profited them that have been occupied therein.**

Because the Bible was written thousands of years ago, we
need help to understand what the Bible is saying to us now.
This is because the language of the Bible differs from what we
know and speak today. Cultures were different then than now.
We must be careful not to interpret everything we read in the
Bible only in light of our own culture.

The Heart of Your Library

At the heart of every good library should be, first of all, a
good study Bible. If you already have a good study Bible you
are comfortable with, you will probably want to continue to use
it. If you do not have a good study Bible, you may want to refer
to the list of study Bibles given in the previous chapter in order
to find one that suits you. It does not matter which version you
use; just use one you are familiar and comfortable with.

The second necessary item in your library is a good concordance. Strong's and Young's are both great if you are studying
out of the *King James Version*. If your study Bible is another
version, you will just need to find out what is the best concordance for your version. Some examples of good concordances in
different versions include, but are not limited to:

1. *The NIV Complete Concordance* by Edward W. Goodrick
and John R. Kohlenberger, III.

2. *The NASB Handy Concordance* published by
Zondervan.

3. *The RSV Handy Concordance* published by Zondervan.

These are just a few of the many that are available. If you
cannot find one in your version, ask at your local Christian
bookstore. Concordances are available in several different versions and formats.

Fine-Tuning Your Library

Once you have a good study Bible and concordance, you are ready to begin adding to your library. You may want to begin by adding one or more of the references we will list in this section. I would strongly recommend, however, that rather than going out and spending a lot of money to buy one or more of everything, you start simple. Take your time. Spend some time browsing through the books you are considering, then purchase only the one(s) that you think will benefit you most right now. Remember, you can always add more later.

The following are some reference books that you may want to consider adding to your library as it grows. This is by no means a complete list, but rather a good starting place. More in-depth information on the reference materials can be found in the section on Bible Study Tools.

1) Bible Handbook(s)

Buying a good Bible Handbook is an excellent way to start building your library. Bible handbooks contain much concise information, usually enough to get you started.

2) Bible Dictionaries

These are quick and easy to use. They can give you a wealth of information about things such as people, places, and events, as well as certain Bible terms and words.

3) Topical Bible(s)

Nave's Topical Bible is the best one that is currently readily available. You can, however, run across some other very good ones in used bookstores.

4) Word Study Aids

Word study books are good for bringing out the meanings of words in more detail. They are written so that they are easy to understand. One does not have to know how to read Greek or Hebrew to use them.

5) Bible Atlases

Bible Atlases are particularly valuable for studying the lives of individuals either in the Old or New Testament. They are also very helpful for studying locations and regions.

6) Commentaries

When choosing a commentary, you may want to refer to the list of commentaries given in the chapter on Bible Study Tools. It is also helpful to talk with someone who owns a certain commentary or commentaries that you are considering. Look through it. Learn something of the background of the writer(s) of the commentary that you are considering. Remember that you will not agree one hundred percent with everything that every commentator has to say.

7) Theology Books

Although the term "Theology Book" sounds foreboding, remember it is not referring only to those big, hard-to-understand books that we so often equate with theology books. Theology, in its simplest form, means a study of or about God. A theology book could be a book by E. W. Kenyon, Kenneth Copeland or any other author whose "theology" you feel is sound.

8) Parallel Bibles

Parallel Bibles are Bibles that give more than one translation in a parallel format to make verse comparisons easy. They can have as few as two or as many as eight translations in one volume.

9) Miscellaneous Volumes

Treasury of Scripture Knowledge by R. A. Torrey:

If you use the center reference of your Bible a lot, then I would recommend that you look into the layout of this book. It is a full-size book of nothing but cross-references.

The New Testament from 26 Translations / The Bible from 26 Translations:

A good start on a translation notebook. Although it can never take the place of the one that you compile, it does have translation comparisons on almost every verse. These books can be very useful for a quick look at how the different versions render a particular verse or passage.

Adding Translations to Your Library

All serious Bible students can benefit from using more than one translation of the Bible. Bible translations are helpful in that they can shed light on difficult passages and help us to see Scripture from a fresh perspective.

When looking for translations to add to your personal library, keep in mind that there are several types of translations, each with a different purpose. I would suggest that you have several translations in a variety of types. Each type of translation has merit and is useful for study, and each type will contribute to your Bible study in a different way. The following is a list of the different types of Bible translations available.

1) Ultraliteral Translations

Ultraliteral translations are translations which attempt to provide an English word for every Greek or Hebrew word in the original text, in other words, a word-for-word translation of the original. These are usually very difficult to read but can be very helpful for finding exact word meanings, etc.

2) Literal translations

Literal translations are those which provide in a readable format the English word or phrase equivalent for each word or phrase used in the original text.

3) Modern Literal translations

Modern Literal translations substitute modern words for archaic words, bringing the Bible into a modern language yet still retaining the literal form.

4) Modern English translations

These present a rendering of the text in present-day English and contemporary style.

5) Paraphrases

Paraphrases are expanded translations, attempting to provide the meaning of the original not word for word, but rather thought for thought, bringing out the rich shades of meaning in the original words.

6) Simple English translations

The main emphasis of a Simple English translation is to make it easy to read and understand. Only common words are used and long sentences are broken into shorter ones.

7) Narrative translations

Narrative versions retell the text in a story form, which is especially useful for reading aloud in family devotions.

To further illustrate the value of translations for study, we will now look at the last part of Acts 17:22 in a variety of translations.

Literal Translations

ACTS 17:22
22 .... I perceive that in all things ye are too superstitious.

ACTS 17:22 (ASV)
... I perceive that ye are very religious.

ACTS 17:22 (Worrell)
... in all respects I observe that ye are more than usually regardful of the deities.

ACTS 17:22 (*Young*)
. . . in all things I perceive you as over-religious.

ACTS 17:22 (*Rotherham*)
. . . In every way, how unusually reverent of the demons ye are I perceive.

ACTS 17:22 (*NKJV*)
. . . I perceive that in all things you are very religious.

ACTS 17:22 (*RSV*)
. . . I perceive that in every way you are very religious.

ACTS 17:22 (*Bowes*)
. . . I perceive you are exceedingly addicted to the worship of invisible powers.

ACTS 17:22 (*Anderson*)
. . . I perceive that in all respects your reverence for demons excels that of other men.

ACTS 17:22 (*Murdock*)
. . . I perceive that in all things ye are excessive in the worship of demons.

ACTS 17:22 (*Newcome*)
. . . I perceive that ye are exceedingly addicted to the worship of demons.

ACTS 17:22 (*Sawyer*)
. . . I perceive that in all things you are extremely devoted to the worship of demons.

ACTS 17:22 (*Green*)
. . . in all things I remark that you are much in awe of higher powers.

Modern Literal Translations

ACTS 17:22 (*NASB*)
. . . I observe that you are very religious in all respects.

ACTS 17:22 (*NAB*)
... I note that in every respect you are scrupulously religious.

ACTS 17:22 (*NIV*)
... I see that in every way you are very religious.

Modern English Translations

ACTS 17:22 (*Berkeley*)
... I notice on every hand how religious you are.

ACTS 17:22 (*New Jerusalem Bible*)
... I have seen for myself how extremely scrupulous you are in all religious matters.

ACTS 17:22 (*Knox*)
... wherever I look I find you scrupulously religious.

ACTS 17:22 (*Williams*)
... at every turn I make I see that you are very religious.

ACTS 17:22 (*Phillips*)
... my own eyes tell me that you are in all respects an extremely religious people.

ACTS 17:22(*NEB*)
... I see that in everything that concerns religion you are uncommonly scrupulous.

ACTS 17:22(*Goodspeed*)
... from every point of view I see that you are extremely religious.

ACTS 17:22(*Beck*)
... I see how very religious you are in every way.

ACTS 17:22 (*Moffatt*)
... I observe at every turn that you are a most religious people.

ACTS 17:22 (*Weymouth New Testament*)
. . . I perceive that you are in every respect remarkably religious.

ACTS 17:22 (*Tentative Edition*)
. . . on every hand I see signs of your being very devout.

ACTS 17:22 (*TEV*)
. . . I see that in every way you Athenians are very religious.

ACTS 17:22 (*Barclay*)
. . . I cannot help seeing that generally speaking you tend to be a very religious people.

Simple English Translations

ACTS 17:22 (*New Century Bible*)
. . . I can see that you are very religious in everything.

ACTS 17:22 (Simple English Bible)
. . . I can see that you are very religious in all things.

ACTS 17:22 (*Cressman*)
. . . I see that you worship too many gods.

Paraphrases

ACTS 17:22 (*The Living Bible*)
. . . I notice that you are very religious.

ACTS 17:22 (*Baxter*)
. . . Ye are on pretense of being very religious, addicted to worship multitudes of gods.

ACTS 17:22 (*Lovett*)
. . . I see that when it comes to religion you are scrupulous in every detail.

ACTS 17:22 (*Hammond*)
. . . Ye Athenians have a greater number of gods
which ye worship, than any other cities have, margin — I look upon you, as those which are generally given to the worship of more Gods, or demons,
than any.

Study Bibles

What is a study Bible?

Study Bibles are Bibles which have study notes either in
the margin (or elsewhere), or inserted into the text. Many
study Bibles are available in several popular versions. The following is a list of good study Bibles that are readily available.
There are others, of course, but these are some of the more
popular ones.

The Open Bible

Available in *King James, New King James*, and *New
American Standard Versions, The Open Bible* has alternate
renderings and cross references at the end of selected verses.
It also offers good footnotes that correspond to an outline at
the beginning of the Bible, which is suitable for new believers
and basic foundations. It contains many good helps in the
back, as well as a Biblical Cyclopedic Index.

Thompson Chain Reference

Available in *King James* and *New International Versions*,
the *Thompson Chain Reference Bible* has extensive chain references found in the margin which are keyed to a listing in the
back. The list in the back does not contain all references found
in the text. This Bible has more helps than any other Bible,
too many to list here.

Ryrie Study Bible

This Bible is available in *King James, New King James,
New American Standard* and *New International Versions*. It

contains many good footnotes, but leans heavily toward the Baptist doctrine.

NIV Study Bible

Available in *New International Version* only, the *New International Version Study Bible* has extensive notes. It is a good study Bible if you use the *New International Version*.

Scofield Reference Bible

Scofield's Bible is available in *King James Version* only. It has a good chain reference, as well as extensive footnotes.

The New Scofield Reference Bible

The New Scofield Bible is available in *King James Version* (with slight variation on the text), *New International Version*, *New King James Version*, and *New American Standard Bible*. It has the best system for chain reference, better than the earlier Scofield and even better than Thompson's chain reference, although it does not have as many listings. It has extensive footnotes (notes vary from earlier edition), and alternate renderings to update the *King James* (*King James Version only*).

Dake's Annotated Reference Bible

Available in *King James Version* only, this Bible has very extensive notes with some very good notes on healing.

New Analytical Bible (Dickson Bible)

Available in *King James Version* only, the *New Analytical Bible* has inserted in the text in brackets alternate renderings from the *American Standard Version, 1901 Standard Edition*. It also contains an outline of each book at the end of the last chapter of that book, followed by outstanding facts. Many good features can be found in the back, such as chronological notes, notes on the lives of several outstanding men of the Bible, a topical study of the Bible, and more.

Full Life Study Bible

The *Full Life Study Bible* is available in *King James* and *New International Versions*. This is a very good study Bible with Pentecostal and Charismatic notes. It seems to be one of the best so far.

The Word Bible

Available in *King James* only. This is a good one to use for reading through as well as studying from since all the notes are in the back. Unique markers are found in the margin for the notes in the back. It contains many excellent articles from various well-known authors.

RHEMA Study Bible

Available in *King James Version* only, the *RHEMA Study Bible* contains a Biblical Cyclopedic Index and a cross reference with alternate renderings.

Spirit Filled Life Bible

Available in *New King James Version* only, it is the work of more than sixty contributors. This Bible contains twenty-two Bible topics listed under the heading of "Kingdom Dynamics." It has more than 550 key words from the Greek and Hebrew language. They are all keyed to Strong's numbering system. It also has several good in-text maps and charts as well as a good center reference and many other good features.

Translations As Study Bibles

Although not to be confused with study Bibles, many translations make good study Bibles because of the way in which they were translated. The following is a list of translations that make good study Bibles.

The Amplified Bible

This translation brings out shades of meaning and nuances that are not possible in a word-for-word rendering. It is a good study Bible because key words are "amplified."

Expanded Translation of the New Testament by **Kenneth S. Wuest**

Follows the Greek word order and is expanded to bring out word meanings. It is different from *The Amplified Bible* in that the text flows smoothly with the thought of using as many English words as necessary to convey the Greek thought. It is especially good on verb tenses.

Concordant Literal

The Concordant Literal translation attempts to use one English word for each Greek word while taking context into consideration. Is good for study because it is very literal and true to the Greek.

Translator's New Testament

The Translator's New Testament was originally used to help translators translate from English into other languages. It has extensive translational helps in the back.

Where and How To Build Your Library

The first and probably the easiest place to start looking for materials is your local Christian bookstore. Be sure to watch for special sales and close-out sales. Remember that just because a book is being closed out does not mean that it is not a useful study tool. Stores usually close out books because they have set on the shelf too long and the average person does not want them. If you can use it and can afford it, then consider buying it for your library.

Another very good source for finding study material is a used bookstore. This is often a good place to find the materials you want at a reduced price. You can often find used copies of the books you want at a fraction of the price. Used bookstores are also good for finding out-of-print items. Prices may vary greatly from one bookstore to another, so do not get upset if you find the same book in one store for less than what you paid for it in another store the week before. If it was a good buy then, it probably still is. Remember that you may not run across that same book again for a long time.

There are a few good mail order houses. Your pastor or Bible teacher will probably know of some, so you may want to ask them.

Using Your Library

Making translation notebooks is a very profitable way of studying. With this method you are studying the Word of God itself. This study method will bring things alive to you that will enhance your spiritual growth in a phenomenal way.

Begin by taking a verse or portion of a verse and writing it down. (Hint: It is best to begin your comparison with the *King James Version*. This is helpful if you want to use another study book along with your translation notebook, and the study book is based on the *King James Version*, as most are.) Then, simply begin looking for additional translations of the verse you are studying and write them down. Use only translations or versions that speak to you concerning the verse that you are adding to your notebook. In most cases it is best to write out the whole verse. You can make a translation notebook by using the main portions of a particular book of the Bible, by using a particular topic, or just by writing down verses that have meant a lot to you over the years.

Studying them from new translations will give you a fresh insight into those well-loved verses. You will want to be sure to start each verse on a new piece of paper. This way you can add more translations to your notebook as you need to in the future. You will also be able to place your verses in a consecutive order.

Using Your Library Devotionally

Many of your study tools can be used as devotional helps. For example, you might find reading through a commentary by Matthew Henry or Kenneth Wuest to be very devotional. Some of these older writers had a very close relationship with the Lord that shows up in their writings. Often as you read through them, you will find yourself caught up in that same atmosphere. Do not be afraid to mark or highlight in your books. This will help you to find the passages that have blessed you.

Sermon books by such time tested authors are also a good source of devotional reading. Do not be too concerned about what denomination the writer is. If he is truly a man of God, he will have some good things to say that could be a real blessing.

Summary

Remember, this is only a set of suggestions to help get you started. Do not be concerned if your method of study is not like that of someone else. The important thing is that you get the Word of God in your heart. Realize that the average Christian does not even read his Bible on a daily basis. Therefore, whatever you do is better than average if you are doing it on a regular basis. Also remember to always pray before you begin to study, inviting the Holy Spirit to become involved.

Building a library is a lifetime affair. There is no need to be in a hurry to acquire a large library all at once. Rather, learn to use each study tool effectively as you get it, then consider what you need to add next. (Note: A person called to the ministry of a teacher, however, may find it necessary to build his or her library more quickly than the average Christian. Also, when studying a particular topic such as prayer, healing, the life of Jesus or parables, you may need to acquire several books at once on that topic.)

Do not forget that it is also helpful to read the writings of others. There is a great wealth of information to be obtained in books. To not read writings by different authors is almost like saying that God speaks to no one but you.

You should feed regularly on such topics as love, humility, and the fruit of the Spirit. These will help you to keep a proper perspective. We study the Bible to bring us closer to our Lord Jesus Christ, never to give us a superior attitude over others. Colossians 2:7 in *The Letters of St. Paul*, by Arthur Way, says, "Be like trees fast-rooted, like buildings steadily rising, feeling His presence about you, and ever (for to this your education has led up) unshaken in your faith, and overflowing with thanksgiving."

Chapter 8
Bible Study Tools

ACTS 8:30b,31a (*TEV*)
Do you understand what you are reading? . . . How
can I understand unless someone explain it to me?

In this chapter we will be looking at different study tools
that you can use to help you gain a better understanding of
God's Word. We will be looking at several different types of
study tools. This list of study tools is by no means exhaustive.
I have only picked out the ones that are easy to come by as
well as easy to use, that you will be able to get the most out of.
You may wish to refer back to this chapter when deciding
which study tools you want to add to your library, or when
learning to use your new study tools.

Bible Handbooks

A Bible handbook is, in essence, a concise Bible commentary, a Bible dictionary, and a Bible atlas in a single volume.
Bible handbooks give quick and easy information, which
makes them very useful for personal devotions.

What is the principle use of a Bible handbook? The major
portion of most Bible handbooks consists of an abbreviated
Bible commentary, including introductions to and outlines of
each Book of the Bible, summaries of each chapter, and explanations of difficult passages.

Bible handbooks contain articles on many biblical topics
such as biblical archaeology, governments and politics, biblical

customs and times, coinage, weights and measurements, and weapons and warfare.

Some Bible handbooks include helpful photographs, maps, charts, and so forth. These give helpful information in the Old Testament on kings, prophets, and so forth, and are especially helpful in the New Testament when studying the four Gospels and the Book of Revelation.

Some suggested Bible Handbooks:

1) *Halley's Bible Handbook*, by Henry Halley. Very popular, over four million in print. Very comprehensive. Available in paperback, hardback, and large print.

2) *Unger's Bible Handbook*, by Merrill F. Unger. A small, inexpensive, chapter-by-chapter reference book.

3) *Abingdon Bible Handbook*, by Edward P. Blair. Very good for photographs and maps, contains an insert on the Holy Land.

4) *The Bible Almanac*, ed. by J. I. Packer, Merrill Tenney, and William White Jr. Instead of being divided by Books of the Bible, it is divided by forty-six Bible topics.

5) *Eerdman's Handbook to the Bible*, edited by David and Pat Alexander. Divided into four sections: general information on the Bible, the Old Testament, the New Testament, and special articles on specific Bible topics. Includes hundreds of color maps, charts, and photographs.

6) *Eerdman's Handbook to the History of Christianity*, by Tim Dowley. Consisting of over 600 pages. Very good for a general view of Christian history.

7) *Blaiklock's Handbook to the Bible*, by E. M. Blaiklock. A very concise look at each Book of the Bible.

Bible Dictionaries

A Bible dictionary gives detailed information about persons, places, events, and certain Bible terms and words. It can provide a wealth of information quickly and easily.

Which Bible dictionaries should I use? There are many different ones, all of them good, that you can choose from. I suggest starting with one that fits your budget as well as your need. You should, over a period of time, have two or three good Bible dictionaries in your library. They are all different.

Bible Commentaries

A Bible commentary is a reference book devoted to the explanation, illustration, and sometimes the homiletic (art of preaching) expansion of the text of some portion of Scripture. They can be one volume or many volumes. They may contain the original Greek or Hebrew text, or English text. They can be scholarly, technical, and critical.

Some Suggested Commentaries

Single volume commentaries on individual Books of the Bible: for example, Romans, Hebrews, or Revelation by William Newell.

Single volume commentaries on the whole Bible: for example, *The One Volume Bible Commentary* by J. R. Durnmelow, or *A Commentary Critical and Explanatory on the Whole Bible* by Jamieson, Fausset, and Brown.

Multiple volumes on either the whole Bible or just the New Testament: for example, *Matthew Henry's Commentary*, an excellent commentary for the whole Bible. Also, for the New Testament, the *Tyndale New Testament Commentaries*, *The Daily Study Bible* by William Barclay, and *Barnes' Notes on the New Testament* (this can be contained in single or multiple volumes).

There is an Old Testament Commentary set worth mentioning here, the *Commentary on the Old Testament* by Carl Keil and Franz Delitzsch. It contains a literal translation of the Scriptures. Its notes, however, are sometimes very technical.

Keep in mind that many of the multi-volume sets can be bought one at a time, making them easier to obtain.

Bible Study Reference Books

Bible study reference books are written for the student who knows little or no Greek. They are usually easy to understand and easy to use. They offer information on the history of words as well as idioms used in Bible times. They are often useful for finding different shades or pictures of a word.

Some suggested Bible Study Reference Books:

1) *Word Studies in the Greek New Testament* by Kenneth Wuest. Three volumes hardback or multi-volume paperback. Looks at several New Testament books verse by verse, as well as topics and certain words. Volume four is the *Expanded New Testament*.

2) *Vincent's Word Studies of the New Testament* by Marvin Vincent. A four volume set going through the entire New Testament commenting on certain words and phrases.

3) *Word Meanings in the New Testament* by Ralph Earle. Like Vincent, Earle goes through the entire New Testament commenting on certain words and phrases. He does not look at as many words, but his comments are very good.

Concordances

A good concordance will be invaluable to you in your study time. We will be looking at the primary uses of concordances and then look specifically at two very popular and useful concordances, Strong's and Young's. These two are based on the *King James Version of the Bible*; however, you can use them to study from another translation if you choose by doing a comparative study beginning with the *King James* first.

For instance, you can look up a word using one of these concordances, then with your translation next to the *King James* you will find a limited amount of scriptures that pertain to the word that you are searching out. This will prove to be only a little better than using the concordance found in the back of most other versions.

What is a concordance? A Bible concordance lists all or many of the words of the Bible in alphabetical order and indicates the chapter and verse where they occur. Some words will have many listings, while others will have only a few. Some concordances are exhaustive, listing every word in the Bible. Others are not.

What can you do with a concordance? One of the primary uses of a concordance is to locate a particular text. They are designed to help you quickly find any Bible verse you may want to locate. You can also look up every occurrence of a particular word.

Because words are given in order of their occurrence, one can learn the complete teaching of:

1) A particular author. Example: The Apostle John in his Gospel.

2) A person on a particular subject. Example: What John has to say about "eternal life."

Bible concordances are also especially helpful for finding word definitions, as well as for comparing the way a particular Greek or Hebrew word is translated in various passages of Scripture. Especially in the *King James Version*, a particular Greek or Hebrew word is often translated completely differently from one passage to the next. Many words that appear to have the same English meaning actually have different Greek or Hebrew root words, with different meanings. With a good concordance, you can find this root word and find the accurate meaning of the *King James* word as it applies to the passage you are studying.

Recommended Concordances

Strong's Exhaustive Concordance of the Bible

Strong's Concordance was first published in 1890 by James Strong. He spent thirty-five years working on it. It includes a complete listing of every word in the *King James Version of the Bible*, with some editions even listing the occurrences of articles such as "a," "an," and "the." Strong's contains concise dictionaries of the Hebrew and Greek words, giving their English meanings. Each word has its own number, which corresponds to the listing in the Hebrew or Greek concordance. This numbering system is unique to Strong's. Dr. Strong originated this system. He keyed the English text of the *King James Version* to the Hebrew and Greek language using numbers. Strong's system is almost universal and is very easy to use. You do not need to know any Hebrew or Greek to use it. In fact, most other references that use a numbering system use Strong's system.

It is interesting to note that the numbers 2717 and 3203 through 3302 are omitted in the New Testament section. This will not cause any inconveniences. In fact many have used Strong's Concordance for years and have never known this.

How to use Strong's Concordance

To find a particular verse:

Pick an outstanding word in the verse you want to find and look it up in the concordance. Then look through the given references on that word and find the verse you are wanting. For instance, if you were looking for John 14:2, you would not want to use the word "house" to find the verse. There are 2,024 listings of the word "house." Trying to find it that way could take a while. However, the word "mansions" is a more outstanding word. When you look up that word you will find your passage much more quickly.

To find a word definition:

After locating the passage of Scripture containing the word you want to look up in the concordance section, locate the number listed to the right. I would strongly suggest that you write this number down on a piece of paper, especially if you will be looking up more than one word. This will keep you from having to go back again if you forget the number. For most people, these numbers start to run together after a while.

Next look up the number in the dictionary section. Note the separate dictionaries for Hebrew (Old Testament) and Greek (New Testament). Many times people look up their word in the wrong dictionary, and think that they have a very unusual meaning to the word that they have found. For some reason Dr. Strong used normal character letters when referring to the Old Testament section, and italics when he referred to the New Testament.

The dictionary section is set up as in the example that follows:

652 (apostolos, *ap-ós-tol-os*; from *649*; a *delegate*; spec. an *ambassador* of the Gospel; officially a *commissioner* of Christ ["*apostle*"] (with miraculous powers): — apostle, messenger, he that is sent.

The first word is the literal Greek or Hebrew word.

The second word we find, "apostolos", is a transliteration of the Greek (or Hebrew) word (English equivalent of the Greek or Hebrew letters).

The third word we find, "ap-ós-tol-os", is the pronunciation of the Greek (or Hebrew) word.

Next we see the number of the root word, from 649, that our word is derived from, if there is a root word.

Now we come to the concise meaning of our word with the definition going up to the colon (:), *a delegate*; spec. an *ambassador* of the Gospel; officially a *commissioner* of Christ [*"apostle"*] (with miraculous powers):

Any word found to the right of the colon is not part of the definition. Rather, it shows the various ways that the *King James* translators have rendered this word, in this case — "apostle, messenger, he that is sent."

Strong's Dictionary Symbols — Greek New Testament

abst. = abstract(-ly)

acc. = accusative (case)

adv. = adverb(-ial)(-ly)

aff. = affinity

alt. = alternate(-ly)

anal. = analogy

app. = apparent(-ly)

caus. = causative(-ly)

cer. = ceremony, ceremonial(-ly)

Chald. = Chaldee

Chr. = Christian

coll. = collective(-ly)

comp. = comparative, compare, comparatively,
          compound(-s)

concr. = concrete(-ly)

corr. = corresponding

dat. = dative (case)

der. = derivation, derivative, derived

dim. = diminutive

dir. = direct(-ly)

E. = East

eccl. = ecclesiastical(-ly)

Eg. = Egypt(ian)

ell. = ellipsis, elliptical(-ly)

eq. = equivalent

esp. = especially

euph. = euphemism, euphemistic, euphemistically

ext. = extension

fem. = feminine

fig. = figurative(-ly)

for. = foreign

gen. = genitive (case)

Gr. = Greek

Heb. = Hebraism, Hebrew

i.e. = id est, that is

imper. = imperative

imperf. = imperfect

impers. = impersonal(-ly)

impl. = implication, implied

incl. = including

ind. = indicative(-ly)

indiv. = individual(-ly)

inf. = infinitive

inh. = inhabitant(-s)

intens. = intensive(-ly)

intr. = intransitive(-ly)

invol. = involuntary, involuntarily

irr. = irregular(-ly)

Isr. = Israelite(-s), Israelitish

Jer. = Jerusalem

Lat. = Latin

lit. = literal(-ly)

mean. = meaning

ment. = mental(-ly)

mid. = middle (voice)

mor. = moral(-ly)

mult. = multiplicative

nat. = natural(-ly)

neg. = negative(-ly)

neut. = neuter

obj. = objective(-ly)

obs. = obsolete

or. = origin(-al)(-ly)

Pal. = Palestine

part. = participle

pass. = passive(-ly)

perh. = perhaps

pers. = person(-al)(-ly)

phys. = physical(-ly)

pl. = plural

pos. = positive(-ly)

pref. = prefix(-ed)

prim. = primary

prob.= probably

prol. = prolongation, prolonged

pron. = pronominal(-ly), pronoun

prop. = properly

redupl. = reduplicated, reduplication

refl. = reflexive(-ly)

rel. = relative(-ly)

Rom. = Roman

sing. = singular

spec. = special

subj. = subjective(-ly)

sup. = superlative(-ly)

tech. = technical(-ly)

term. = termination

trans. = transitive(-ly)

transp. = transposed, transposition

typ. = typical(-ly)

unc. = uncertain

var. = variation, various

voc. = vocative

vol. = voluntarily, voluntary

Signs Employed

+ (addition) — Denotes a rendering in the *Authorized Version* (AV) of one or more Greek words in connection with the one under consideration.

X (multiplication) — Denotes a rendering in the AV that results from an idiom peculiar to the Greek.

( ) (parenthesis) — In the renderings from the AV, denotes a word or syllable sometimes given in connection with the principal word to which it is annexed.

[ ] (bracket) — In the rendering from the AV, denotes the inclusion of an additional word in the Greek.

Comments — At the end of a rendering from the AV, denotes an explanation of the variations from the usual form.

Strong's Dictionary Symbols — Hebrew Bible

abb. = abbreviated, abbreviation

absol. = absolute, absolutely

abstr. = abstract, abstractly

act. = active, actively

adj. = adjective, adjectively

adv. = adverb, adverbial, adverbially

aff. = affix, affixed

affin. = affinity

appar. = apparent, apparently

arch. = architecture, architectural, architecturally

art. = article

artif. = artificial, artificially

Ass. = Assyrian

A.V. = Authorized Version

Bab. = Babylon, Babylonia, Bablylonian

caus. = causative, causatively

Chald. = Chaldaism, Chaldee

collat. = collateral, collaterally

collect. = collective, collectively

comp. = compare, comparative, comparatively, comparison

concr. = concrete, concretely

conjec. = conjecture, conjectural, conjecturally

conjug. = conjugation, conjugational, conjugationally

conjuc. = conjunction, conjunctional, conjunctionally

constr. = construct, construction, constructive, constructively

contr. = contracted, contraction

correl. = corelated, correlation, correlative, correlatively

corresp. = corresponding, correspondingly

def. = definite, definitely

denom. = denominative, denominately

der. = derivation, derivative, derivatively

desc. = descendant, descendants

E. = East, Eastern

e.g. = exempli gratia, for example

Eg. = Egypt, Egyptian, Egyptians

ellip. = ellipsis, elliptical, elliptically

equiv. = equivalent, equivalently

err. = erroneous, erroneously, error

esp. = especial, especially

etym. = etymology, etymological, etymologically

euphem. = euphemism, euphemistic, euphemistically

euphon. = euphonically, euphonious

extern. = external, externally

infer. = inference, inferential, inferentially

fem. = feminine

fig. = figurative, figuratively

for. = foreign, foreigner

freq. = frequentative, frequentatively

fut. = future

gen. = general, generally, genetical, generically

Gr. = Graecism, Greek

gut. = guttural

Heb. = Hebraism, Hebrew

i.e. = id est, that is

ident. = identical, identically

immed. = immediate, immediately

imper. = imperative, imperatively

impl. = implication, implied, impliedly

incept. = inceptive, inceptively

incl. = including, inclusive, inclusively

indef. = indefinite, indefinitely

infin. = infinitive

inhab. = inhabitant, inhabitants

ins. = inserted

intens. = intensive, intensively

intern. = internal, internally

interj. = interjection, interjectional, interjectionally

intr. = intransitive, intransitively

Isr. = Israelite, Israelites, Israelitish

Jerus. = Jerusalem

Levit. = Levitical, Levitically

lit. = literal, literally

marg. = margin, marginal (reading)

masc. = masculine

mean. = meaning

ment. = mental, mentally

mid. = middle

modif. = modified, modification

mor. = moral, morally

mus. = musical

nat. = native, natural, naturally, nature

neg. = negative, negatively

obj. = object, objective, objectively

or. = origin, original, originally

orth. = orthography, orthographical, orthographically

Pal. = Palestine

part. = participle

pass. = passive, passively

patron. = patronymic, patronymically

perh. = perhaps

perm. = permutation (of allied letters)

pers. = person, personal, personally

Pers. = Persia, Persian, Persians

phys. = physical, physically

plur. = plural

poet. = poetry, poetical, poetically

pos. = positive, positively

pref. = prefix, prefixed

prep. = preposition, prepositional, prepositionally

prim. = primitive

prob. = probable, probably

prol. = prolonged, prolongation

pron. = pronominal, pronominally, pronoun

prox. = proximate, proximately

rad. = radical

recip. = reciprocal, reciprocally

redupl. = reduplicated, reduplication

refl. = reflexive, reflexively

rel. = relative, relatively

relig. = religion, religious, religiously

second. = secondarily, secondary

signif. = signification, signifying

short. = shortened, shorter

sing. = singular

spec. = specific, specifically

streng. = strengthening

subdiv. = subdivision, subdivisional, subdivisionally

subj. = subject, subjective, subjectively

substit. = substituted

superl. = superlative, superlatively

symb. = symbolical, symbolically

tech. = technical, technically

tran. = transitive, transitively

transc. = transcription

transp. = transposed, transposition

unc. = uncertain, uncertainly

var. = variation

Signs Employed

+ (addition) — Denotes a rendering in the *Authorized Version* (AV) of one or more Hebrew words in connection with the one under consideration.

X (multiplication) — Denotes a rendering in the AV that results from an idiom peculiar to the Hebrew.

° (degree) — Appended to a Hebrew word, denotes a vowel-pointing corrected from that of the text. (This mark is set in Hebrew Bibles over syllables in which the vowels of the margin have been inserted instead of those properly belonging to the text.)

( ) (parenthesis) — In the renderings from the AV, denotes a word or syllable sometimes given in connection with the principal annexed.

[ ] (bracket) — In the rendering from the AV, denotes the inclusion of an additional word in the Hebrew.

Comments — At the end of a rendering from the AV, denotes an explanation of the variations from the usual form.

Young's Analytical Concordance to the Bible

Young's Concordance was first compiled in 1873. It is called "Analytical" because it groups together the various Greek or Hebrew words which are translated into the same English word.

How To Use Young's Concordance

Begin by looking up the English word you want to know about. They are arranged alphabetically. Each Greek or Hebrew word that has been translated that way will be listed. At the beginning of each group, a literal meaning of the Greek or Hebrew word is given, and then the transliteration of the word. Next are listed the scripture references in which this word is used. Through this method, we can do a fairly accurate word study without knowledge of the original Greek or Hebrew.

An example from *Young's Concordance*:

SUBJECT (to or unto, to be or make) —

1. *Held in, subject or liable to enochos.*

  Heb. 2.15 were all their lifetime subject to bondage

2.   *To set in array under*, hupotassō.

Luke 2.51 was subject unto them: but his mother

10.17 even the devils are subject unto us thro.

10.20 rejoice not, that the spirits are subject u.

Rom. 8.7 for it is not subject to the law of God, ne.

SUBJECT, to —

To set in array, hupotassō.

Rom. 8.20 by reason of him who hath subjected

The first line gives us the word that we are looking for. Notice that the word "subject" has been translated *subject, subject to, subject unto, subject to be*, or *make subject*. Then in the next line we sometimes have a number beginning the line. The amount of numbers that are in a definition tells us the number of different Greek or Hebrew words that have been translated from the word that we are looking up. In the example above we find two different Greek words that have been translated "subject." Next we see some words in italics. This is a brief definition of the Greek or Hebrew word that we are looking at. In the first listing in our example, the definition is *held in subject, subject to*, and *liable to*.

This word is translated "subject" only one time in the *King James Version* of the New Testament. Actually, this Greek word has been translated "guilty of" four times "in danger of" five times and "subject to" only once. Next is listed the actual Greek or Hebrew word, followed by its transliterated equivalent.

At the back of the book are found two index-lexicons, one for the Old Testament and one for the New Testament. They give the original Greek or Hebrew alphabetically and list the ways the word was translated in the *King James Version* and the number of times it was so translated. Several editions also contain an outline of the Books of the Bible.

Word Study Aids

Word study aids are reference tools used to find the meaning of a word or phrase. They are generally available in either New Testament only or Old Testament only.

New Testament Word Study Aids

Thayer's Lexicon

Thayer's Lexicon is very valuable for showing a rich variety of meanings that a word can have. It shows with fine precision how a word can be used in context.

How To Use Thayer's

Be sure to get an edition that is coded to Strong's. First, you will want to find Strong's number for the word you want to look up either in Strong's Concordance or in an interlinear New Testament that uses Strong's numbering system. Next, locate that number in the margin of Thayer's. Now you can read the English meaning of the word you looked up. It is helpful to scan through the text, which can sometimes be lengthy, and find the verse in which your word is found. I have found that using a plain colored card or piece of paper to cover the lines below the one that I am reading makes this work much easier.

The most accurate definition for the word as it is used in this verse can be found preceding this verse reference. The asterisk (*) at the end of the definition means that all of the listings of that word in the *King James Version* have been referred to.

Bullinger's Critical Concordance to the English and Greek New Testament

Bullinger's Concordance gives the English words in their alphabetical order. All verbs are listed in their present tense.

How To Use Bullinger's

In Bullinger's, each word is set in its own section. The definition is listed first, and a concordance for the English word follows. If the word has been translated from more than one Greek word, go to the concordance of the word and locate the number to the left. Then go back to the definition section to that number, and you will find your definition.

There is a Greek-English index in the back. This lists words in the order of the Greek alphabet. It also lists the different ways the Greek word has been translated in the *King James Version* and how many times.

Three appendices are also contained in the back. These are very technical, perhaps too technical for most students.

Appendix A — Various readings in larger clauses.

This appendix gives various readings from a group of different Greek texts.

Appendix B — Parts of speech.

This appendix gives the Greek alphabet, parts of speech, and so forth. Designed for the more scholarly reader.

Appendix C — Variations of the Codex Sinaiticus.

The Codex Sinaiticus was discovered in the Convent of St. Catherine at the foot of Mount Sinai. Constantin von Tischendorf uncovered it during his search in 1844. Bullinger gives a two column table of the variations with the *Authorized Version* (*King James Version*) on the left side and the Critical Readings (Codex Sinaiticus given in English) on the right side. Scripture reference is given on the extreme left side.

Vine's Expository Dictionary of Biblical Words *(New Testament)*

Vine's sometimes shows the precise historical meaning of a word, and other times shows the spiritual significance of a word. It is good for bringing out subtle nuances that a word can have. It is expository, with comments given on various passages referred to under their different headings. Notes are provided on historical, technical, and etymological doctrines.

How To Use Vine's

First, look up the English word. They are listed in alphabetical order. The word is then broken down into categories according to its parts of speech (nouns, verbs, and so forth). In each of these categories, listed by number, are the various transliterated Greek words for that particular English word. Next is the literal Greek word and Strong's number. The definition, along with a partial scripture reference, is given. The fact that the list of scripture references is at times incomplete can be a big drawback to this work.

How will you know which meaning is the one that you are looking for if you can't find your verse? You can, however, by using this newer edition, look up your Strong's number first, then find it in your category. If a paragraph sign (¶) is given, this means that a complete scripture reference has been given.

Old Testament Word Study Aids

Gesenius' Lexicon

Gesenius' Lexicon was first published in 1847. Some of the newer editions are coded to Strong's numbers. It is similar in the Old Testament to Thayer's in the New.

How To Use a Gesenius' Lexicon

To use the edition with Strong's numbers, locate Strong's number corresponding to the word you are looking for. Then find the number in the margin of your Gesenius'. The definition is given beside it.

Wilson's Old Testament Word Studies

This was originally called *The Bible Student's Guide To The More Correct Understanding Of The English Translation*

Of The Old Testament By Reference To The Original Hebrew. It is similar in the Old Testament to Bullinger's in the New.

How To Use a Wilson's

Words are listed alphabetically in English. After the English word is the definition, and then a concordance to the word. If the word has been translated from more than one Hebrew word, go to the concordance of the word and locate the number to the right. Then go back to the definition section to that number and you will find your definition. The letter listed after the number in the concordance corresponds to the number in the definition, representing the different parts of speech of the Hebrew language. Unless you know something of the Hebrew language this will be meaningless to you. Wilson's is generally more technical than most students will need.

Vine's Expository Dictionary of Biblical Words

(Old Testament)

This book was originally called *Nelson's Expository Dictionary of the Old Testament* because it was published by Thomas Nelson Publishers. It was actually written by Merrill Unger and William White. It was chosen to be part of "Vine's" because it is very similar to Vine's. There is a work by Vine that is called *Vine's Expository Dictionary of Old Testament Words*. This is a separate work and is not a part of what is called Vine's today.

How To Use Vine's Expository Dictionary of Biblical Words

English words are listed alphabetically. Some of the words have been broken down into parts of speech. In these categories are listed selected transliterated Hebrew words that have been translated into that particular English word. The literal Hebrew word is given in parenthesis. The definition is then given in quotations with an expansion of the definition following.

It is often best to use the index to find the page number of the word you are looking for, as a word may sometimes be listed in a tense other than the one you are looking for it under.

Part II

Understanding the Language of the Bible

Chapter 9
Understanding Figures of Speech

Our English language, even in its everyday usage, is a complex form of communication. As everyone knows, people seldom communicate in simple, direct ways. Communication is multi-faceted among the human race, certainly extending beyond the spoken or written word. A glance can communicate volumes between two people. We see this complexity most, however, in our spoken and written language. The English language is full of cultural, social, and even regional influences which are responsible for its many colorful idioms and expressions, peculiar to the country or region of the speaker. And so it is with the languages of the Bible.

Often in Scripture we find that whole texts or passages are written in a figurative sense. A good understanding of the various modes of expression found in the languages of the Bible is necessary for a good understanding of the Bible itself. Let us look now at some of the more common modes of expression used in the Bible languages and cultures.

Allegory

An allegory is simply a story in which people, places, and happenings have another meaning, often instructive. An allegory is always written in figurative speech, so that literal interpretation is difficult. It may be a short passage or a lengthy description. Allegories can be found in abundance all

through the Scriptures. Here are a few examples of allegories
in the Scriptures:

ISAIAH 5:1-7
1   Now will I sing to my wellbeloved a song of my
beloved touching his vineyard. My wellbeloved
hath a vineyard in a very fruitful hill:
2   And he fenced it, and gathered out the stones
thereof, and planted it with the choicest vine, and
built a tower in the midst of it, and also made a
winepress therein: and he looked that it should
bring forth grapes, and it brought forth wild
grapes.
3   And now, O inhabitants of Jerusalem, and men
of Judah, judge, I pray you, betwixt me and my
vineyard.
4   What could have been done more to my vineyard, that I have not done in it? wherefore, when I
looked that it should bring forth grapes, brought it
forth wild grapes?
5   And now go to; I will tell you what I will do to
my vineyard: I will take away the hedge thereof,
and it shall be eaten up; and break down the wall
thereof, and it shall be trodden down:
6   And I will lay it waste: it shall not be pruned,
nor digged; but there shall come up briers and
thorns: I will also command the clouds that they
rain no rain upon it.
7   For the vineyard of the Lord of hosts is the
house of Israel, and the men of Judah his pleasant
plant: and he looked for judgment, but behold
oppression; for righteousness, but behold a cry.

1 CORINTHIANS 3:10-15
10 According to the grace of God which is given
unto me, as a wise masterbuilder, I have laid the
foundation, and another buildeth thereon. But let
every man take heed how he buildeth thereupon.
11 For other foundation can no man lay than that
is laid, which is Jesus Christ.
12 Now if any man build upon this foundation
gold, silver, precious stones, wood, hay, stubble;
13 Every man's work shall be made manifest: for

the day shall declare it, because it shall be revealed by fire; and the fire shall try every man's work of what sort it is.

14 If any man's work abide which he hath built thereupon, he shall receive a reward.

15 If any man's work shall be burned, he shall suffer loss: but he himself shall be saved; yet so as by fire.

EPHESIANS 6:11-17

11 Put on the whole armour of God, that ye may be able to stand against the wiles of the devil.

12 For we wrestle not against flesh and blood, but against principalities, against powers, against the rulers of the darkness of this world, against spiritual wickedness in high places.

13 Wherefore take unto you the whole armour of God, that ye may be able to withstand in the evil day, and having done all, to stand.

14 Stand therefore, having your loins girt about with truth, and having on the breastplate of righteousness;

15 And your feet shod with the preparation of the gospel of peace;

16 Above all, taking the shield of faith, wherewith ye shall be able to quench all the fiery darts of the wicked.

17 And take the helmet of salvation, and the sword of the Spirit, which is the word of God.

JOHN 10:1-16

1 Verily, verily, I say unto you, He that entereth not by the door into the sheepfold, but climbeth up some other way, the same is a thief and a robber.

2 But he that entereth in by the door is the shepherd of the sheep.

3 To him the porter openeth; and the sheep hear his voice: and he calleth his own sheep by name, and leadeth them out.

4 And when he putteth forth his own sheep, he goeth before them, and the sheep follow him: for they know his voice.

5 And a stranger will they not follow, but will flee from him: for they know not the voice of strangers.

6 This parable spake Jesus unto them: but they understood not what things they were which he spake unto them.

7 Then said Jesus unto them again, Verily, verily, I say unto you, I am the door of the sheep.

8 All that ever came before me are thieves and robbers: but the sheep did not hear them.

9 I am the door: by me if any man enter in, he shall be saved, and shall go in and out, and find pasture.

10 The thief cometh not, but for to steal, and to kill, and to destroy: I am come that they might have life, and that they might have it more abundantly.

11 I am the good shepherd: the good shepherd giveth his life for the sheep.

12 But he that is an hireling, and not the shepherd, whose own the sheep are not, seeth the wolf coming, and leaveth the sheep, and fleeth: and the wolf catcheth them, and scattereth the sheep.

13 The hireling fleeth, because he is an hireling, and careth not for the sheep.

14 I am the good shepherd, and know my sheep, and am known of mine.

15 As the Father knoweth me, even so know I the Father: and I lay down my life for the sheep.

16 And other sheep I have, which are not of this fold: them also I must bring, and they shall hear my voice; and there shall be one fold, and one shepherd.

JOHN 6:51-65

51 I am the living bread which came down from heaven: if any man eat of this bread, he shall live for ever: and the bread that I will give is my flesh, which I will give for the life of the world.

52 The Jews therefore strove among themselves, saying, How can this man give us his flesh to eat?

53 Then Jesus said unto them, Verily, verily, I say unto you, Except ye eat the flesh of the Son of man, and drink his blood, ye have no life in you.

54 Whoso eateth my flesh, and drinketh my blood, hath eternal life; and I will raise him up at the last day.

55 For my flesh is meat indeed, and my blood is drink indeed.

56 He that eateth my flesh, and drinketh my blood, dwelleth in me, and I in him.

57 As the living Father hath sent me, and I live by the Father: so he that eateth me, even he shall live by me.

58 This is that bread which came down from heaven: not as your fathers did eat manna, and are dead: he that eateth of this bread shall live for ever.

59 These things said he in the synagogue, as he taught in Capernaum.

60 Many therefore of his disciples, when they had heard this, said, This is an hard saying; who can hear it?

61 When Jesus knew in himself that his disciples murmured at it, he said unto them, Doth this offend you?

62 What and if ye shall see the Son of man ascend up where he was before?

63 It is the spirit that quickeneth; the flesh profiteth nothing: the words that I speak unto you, they are spirit, and they are life.

64 But there are some of you that believe not. For Jesus knew from the beginning who they were that believed not, and who should betray him.

65 And he said, Therefore said I unto you, that no man can come unto me, except it were given unto him of my Father.

Symbols

A symbol is a visible, or natural, object which serves to represent a spiritual concept or truth. For instance, a lion, being considered the king of the beasts, symbolizes royalty in the Scriptures. Symbolical acts seen in the Scripture include such things as water baptism, symbolizing our union with Christ in His death, burial, and Resurrection, and the Lord's supper, which is an outward symbol of our spiritual communion with Christ and our participation in His suffering.

The following is a brief list of symbolic words used in Scripture and what they symbolize.

Adultery: Unfaithfulness of God's people (Jer. 3:8,9; Ezek. 23:37)

Ark: Christ (1 Peter 3:20,21; Heb. 11:7)

Babylon: Idolatry (Rev. 17:13; 18:24)

Bear: An enemy (Prov. 17:12)

Blindness: Unbelief (Rom. 11:25)

Bramble, Thorn, or Thistle: Evil influences (Judges 8:9-15)

Cedar: Strength (Ps. 104:16)

Copper (Bronze): Obstinacy, hardness (Isa. 48:4; Jer. 6:28)

Cross: Sacrifice (Col. 2:14)

Death: Separation from God (Gen. 2:17)

Dog: Impurity and apostasy (Prov. 26:11; Phil. 3:2)

Dove: Gentle influence of the Holy Spirit (Matt. 3:16)

Eagle: Power (Deut. 32:11,12)

Eating: Meditation (Ps. 55:1,2)

Fire: The word of God (Jer. 23:29), Purification (Mal. 3:2)

Fox: Deceit or craftiness (Luke 13:32)

Fruit: The consequences of our actions (Matt. 7:16)

Goats: Evil people (Matt. 25:32,33)

Horn: Power (Deut. 33:17)

Horse: Conquest or dominion (Zech. 10:3)

Incense: Prayer (Ps. 141:2)

Lamp: Light, joy (Rev. 2:5)

Leprosy: Sin (Isa. 1:6)

Light: Knowledge (John 12:35)

Marriage: Covenant with God (Isa. 54:1-6; Rev. 19:7)

Oil: The Holy Spirit (James 5:14)

Rock: Shelter or refuge (Ps. 18:2)

Salt: Preservation, incorruption, permanence (Matt. 5:13)

Shoot, Rod, or Stem: The son or descendant of (Isa. 11:1)

Virgins: Faithful servants not having participated in
      idolatry (Rev. 14:4)

Parables

A parable is a kind of allegory in a story form, illustrating an important truth. Jesus was a master at parable telling. He used them often to illustrate His teaching. He often used parables when teaching His disciples in the presence of His enemies, who, not being certain of their interpretation, could not use His words to come against Him.

Good examples of parables which Jesus used to illustrate various truths can be found in Matthew 13:3-8 (the sower sows the word), Matthew 13:24-30, 36-43 (the parable of the tares), and also the fifteenth chapter of Luke which contains the parables of the lost sheep, the lost coin, and the prodigal son. Of course, there are many others.

Remember the following points when interpreting parables:

1) Seek out the object of the parable. What is being illustrated?

2) Do not try to make every detail of the parable apply exactly. Rather apply only the main features of the parable to the interpretation. You will only get into error if you always try to make every detail mean something, they often do not.

3) Remember that parables merely serve to illustrate doctrine and should not be used as a basis for doctrine.

Proverb

The word "proverb" is derived from the Latin *pro* meaning before, and *verb* meaning word, thus an old or common saying. Most proverbs (in the Book of Proverbs) are written in poetic form. They are short sayings expressing wisdom for everyday living, common sense, or reflections of personal experience or observation. The Book of Proverbs is full of practical wisdom and much can be gleaned from studying it. The purpose of the Book of Proverbs is stated in Proverbs 1:2-6, *"To know wisdom and instruction; to perceive the words of understanding; To receive the instruction of wisdom, justice, and judgment, and equity; To give subtility to the simple, to the young man knowledge and discretion. A wise man will hear, and will increase learning; and a man of understanding shall attain unto wise counsels: To understand a proverb, and the interpretation; the words of the wise, and their dark sayings."*

Outside of the Book of Proverbs, we can find examples of proverbs in other scriptures as well. Here are a few examples from the New Testament.

> **LUKE 4:23**
> 23 And he said unto them, Ye will surely say unto me this proverb, Physician, heal thyself: whatsoever we have heard done in Capernaum, do also here in thy country.

> **MARK 6:4**
> 4 But Jesus said unto them, A prophet is not without honour, but in his own country, and among his own kin, and in his own house.

> **2 PETER 2:22**
> 22 But it is happened unto them according to the true proverb, The dog is turned to his own vomit again; and the sow that was washed to her wallowing in the mire.

When searching for the interpretation of a proverb that is difficult to understand, always study the context, which is often the key to the interpretation of any scripture. If you are unable to understand a given proverb, you may want to seek out help from commentaries, whose authors are familiar with the original languages. Remember that the interpretation of a proverb may lie in a custom or idiom peculiar to the culture and language of the proverb's author.

Paradox

A paradox is a statement or saying which is contrary to appearances, and seems impossible or absurd. Jesus often used paradoxes to startle His hearers into seeing the truth.

Examples:

MATTHEW 23:24
24 Ye blind guides, which strain at a gnat, and swallow a camel.

LUKE 18:25
25 For it is easier for a camel to go through a needle's eye, than for a rich man to enter into the kingdom of God.

MARK 8:35
35 For whosoever will save his life shall lose it; but whosoever shall lose his life for my sake and the gospel's, the same shall save it.

MATTHEW 8:22
22 But Jesus said unto him, Follow me; and let the dead bury their dead.

2 CORINTHIANS 12:10
10 Therefore I take pleasure in infirmities, in reproaches, in necessities, in persecutions, in distresses for Christ's sake: for when I am weak, then am I strong.

Chapter 10
Understanding Types

The Bible, especially the Old Testament, is full of types. A "type" is a natural event, person, object, or institution that foretells symbolically an important, usually spiritual, event or concept that is to come (most are fulfilled in the New Testament). Most Bible types are found in the Old Testament, many of them pointing to Christ and His work. God chose to reveal His Messiah to the Israelites through types. In fact, Christ can be found in every Book of the Bible, often through types.

We can see Christ in all of the ceremonies, laws, and institutions of the Mosaic dispensation. Christ Himself said, *"Your father Abraham rejoiced to see my day: and he saw it, and was glad"* (John 8:56). And again, *"For had ye believed Moses, ye would have believed me: for he wrote of me"* (John 5:46).

Let's look at some types of Christ we find in the Old Testament. The examples listed below are not exhaustive, nor are they complete in all details, but are given to help you understand types.

Adam

We can see that Adam is a type of Christ from the following verse:

> **ROMANS 5:14**
> **14 Nevertheless death reigned from Adam to Moses, even over them that had not sinned after the similitude of Adam's transgression, who is the figure of him that was to come.**

As Adam was tempted by the devil and gave in to tempta-
tion, by contrast Christ, when He was tempted, stood firm on
the Word of God. Both acts affected all of mankind.

> **ROMANS 5:19**
> **19 As by one man's disobedience many were made
> sinners, so by the obedience of one shall many be
> made righteous.**

Isaac

The offering of Isaac for a sacrifice is one of the most per-
fect types of Christ's sacrifice at the Cross that we find in the
Bible. Isaac was Abraham's only son, as Christ is God's only
Son. When Isaac asked his father Abraham, "Where is the
lamb for a burnt offering? Abraham replied God will provide
Himself the lamb" (Gen. 22:7,8).

Christ is revealed in the New Testament as *". . . the Lamb
of God which taketh away the sin of the world"* (John 1:29).
And again as in *". . . the Lamb slain before the foundation of
the world"* (Rev. 13:8). Finally, Abraham sacrifices the ram
caught in the thicket. The ram is needed to complete the type
of Christ. *". . . He is brought as a lamb to the slaughter . . ."* (Isa.
53:7), and *"he shall bear their iniquities"* (Isa. 53:11).

Almost all theologians agree that Mount Moriah and
Mount Calvary are the exact same geographical location. This
reference is a good example of how sometimes one picture cannot complete the type of Christ. The ram is needed here to
complete the picture of Christ in this passage.

Joseph

We can see in Joseph a clear picture of the character and
life of Christ. As Joseph was greatly loved by his father, and

then sold by his brothers for the price of a slave, he entered into the role of a servant. As a servant, he was tempted and yet blameless, was unjustly condemned, bound and numbered with transgressors, then exalted as a prince and savior.

Passover Lamb

Christ is the Passover Lamb of Exodus. *". . . Christ our passover is sacrificed for us: Therefore let us keep the feast . . ."* (1 Cor. 5:7,8). In many types there can be room for doubt, but in this type, we see a sure picture of Jesus.

The Rock Smitten in the Desert

Christ was the smitten rock in the desert. *". . . Thou shalt smite the rock, and there shall come water out of it, that the people may drink . . ."* (Exo. 17:6). We find the New Testament answer to this in: *". . . they drank of that spiritual Rock that followed them: and that Rock was Christ"* (1 Cor. 10:4).

Moses

Moses was a type of Christ. He delivered the people from bondage, and gave them a new law. As Moses was an intercessor for his people, so Christ is our intercessor.

The High Priest

Aaron is a type of the high-priestly duties of Christ. It is easy for most of us to see that we no longer need a high priest in the outward sense, that is, some man to act as mediator between us and God. But is it easy for us to see our need for a mediator in a spiritual sense, that is, Jesus as our mediator?

Do we recognize that we cannot come to God on our own, without Jesus? An understanding of the high priest as a type of Jesus can greatly enhance our relationship with the Father. Unlike Aaron, who was a mere man, Jesus was tempted and remained sinless. He was tempted in all points as you and I. Therefore, He is not without compassion and understanding and is able to present our case before the Father through the redemptive work of the Cross.

The Brazen Serpent

JOHN 3:14
14 And as Moses lifted up the serpent in the wilderness, even so must the Son of man be lifted up.

The serpent was made of brass, which is a double symbol of sin. It would have been easy for us to understand if the Lord had told Moses to lift up a young lamb for all to look upon. But instead, He gives us a type of Jesus being made sin for us.

2 CORINTHIANS 5:21
21 For he hath made him to be sin for us, who knew no sin; that we might be made the righteousness of God in him.

The Day of Atonement

The sin offering made on the day of atonement for the people of Israel involved two goats. These two goats formed one offering, but both were needed to complete the type. One goat was sacrificed for a sin offering. The high priest then entered into the Holy of Holies and sprinkled the mercy seat with its blood. The other goat was the scapegoat which the high priest laid his hands upon, confessing the sins of the people. This goat was then released into the wilderness.

We have a picture here of Jesus both ascending and descending, ascending to take His blood to be offered in the Holy of Holies, and descending into hell as a substitute with the sins of mankind.

Jonah

Jonah's experience in the belly of the whale is a type of the death, burial, and resurrection of Christ.

> **MATTHEW 12:40**
> **40 For as Jonas was three days and three nights in the whale's belly, so shall the Son of man be three days and three nights in the heart of the earth.**

More Types

These are just a few of the many types of Christ that we see in the Old Testament. Types are a very rich field for study. They reveal deep and hidden truths about God's character. We also can see Christ typified in the lives of many Old Testament characters such as Aaron, Abel, David, Joshua, and others.

More Old Testament types that make for interesting study include: Leprosy as a type of sin, Cain as a type of natural man, Abel as a type of spiritual man, Enoch as a type of communion, Abraham representing faith, and so forth.

When studying types in the Old Testament, always look at them in light of the New Testament. The Book of Hebrews, for instance, sheds much light on the type of Christ in the tabernacle (Heb. 9:11-28, 10:6-10). And, in the Gospels, Christ reveals types of Himself as well.

Guidelines to consider when studying types:

1. Study Old Testament types as you find them explained in the New Testament.

2. Remember that a type will not accurately correspond to that which it represents in every detail.

3. Old Testament types were given to confirm and illustrate the events and doctrines of the New Testament, not as a basis for doctrine by themselves.

Chapter 11
Hebraisms

Every known language has its idioms, or modes of expression, that are unique to itself. Since the Old Testament was written in Hebrew, the idioms of the Hebrew language are found scattered throughout our English translations. These are known as Hebraisms. A Hebraism is a feature typical of the Hebrew language that occurs especially in another language.

Though not as prevalent, Hebraisms are also to be found in the New Testament, for although the New Testament was written in Greek, it was primarily written by Jews. They, being Jewish, occasionally used these idioms peculiar to their language in their writings. By keeping these Hebraisms (idioms) always in mind we will be able to discern many unclear points and apparent contradictions.

The following excerpt, taken from *The Cottonpatch Version of Paul's Epistles*[1] by Clarence Jordan, helps to illustrate the value of understanding idioms.

Suppose ... someone would be perfectly understood if he wrote to a friend, We had hot dogs and Coke for lunch, fish and hush puppies for supper, and then sat around shooting the bull until midnight.

But let that letter get lost for about two thousand years, then let some Ph.D try to translate it into a non-English language of A.D. 3967.

If he faithfully translated the words it might run something like this: "We had steaming canines (possibly a small variety

such as the Chihuahua Ed.) and processed coal (the coal was
probably not eaten but used to heat the dogs - Ed.) for the noon
meal, fish and mute, immature dogs (no doubt the defective offspring of the hot dog, with which twentieth-century Americans
were so preoccupied Ed.) for the evening meal, followed by passively engaging until midnight in the brutish sport of bull-
shooting (the bulls were then processed into large sausage
called bologna, which sounded like 'baloney' - Ed.)"

For such exacting scholarship the good doctor may have
won world renown as the foremost authority on twentieth-
century English — without having the slightest idea what
was actually said!

Even worse, imagine the impression his literalism gave
his audience of American food and recreational habits!

The following are some of the examples of Hebraisms
found in the Scriptures.

One very commonly used idiom of the Hebrew language is
to say that someone associated with a certain thing or person
is "the son" or "the child" of it.

> **1 SAMUEL 1:16**
> **16 Count not thine handmaid for a DAUGHTER
> OF BELIAL: for out of the abundance of my com-
> plaint and grief have I spoken hitherto.**

A more modern rendering translates this:

> **1 SAMUEL 1:16 (*NIV*)**
> **Do not take your servant for a WICKED WOMAN; I
> have been praying here out of my great anguish
> and grief.**

> **1 SAMUEL 25:17**
> **17 Now therefore know and consider what thou
> wilt do; for evil is determined against our master,
> and against all his household: for he is such a SON
> OF BELIAL, that a man cannot speak to him.**

1 SAMUEL 25:17 (*NIV*)
Now think it over and see what you can do,
because disaster is hanging over our master and
his whole household. He is such a WICKED MAN
that no one can talk to him.

1 SAMUEL 2:12
12 Now the sons of Eli were SONS OF BELIAL,
they knew not the Lord.

1 SAMUEL 2:12 (*NIV*)
Eli's sons were WICKED MEN; they had no regard
for the Lord.

An additional idiom is also found expressed in these verses.
In the Hebrew language, *Belial* signifies a wicked or worthless
person. Thus, the son or daughter of Belial would be a wicked
or worthless person.

More examples of this idiom carried over into the New
Testament are:

LUKE 10:6
6   And if the SON OF PEACE be there, your peace
shall rest upon it: if not, it shall turn to you again.

Here are three more modern translations that bring out
more clearly the meaning of the idiom used in this verse.

LUKE 10:6 (*Weymouth, 3rd Edition*)
And if there is a LOVER OF PEACE there, your
peace shall rest upon it; otherwise it shall come
back upon you.

LUKE 10:6 (*TCNT — Tentative Edition*)
Then, if any one there PROVES DESERVING OF A
BLESSING, your blessing will stay upon him; but if
not, it will come back upon yourselves.

LUKE 10:6 (*P. G. Parker*)
And if a PEACEFUL MAN is there, then God's
peace will rest upon his house; but if not, God's

peace will remain with you and not be distributed to that house.

Here, the "son of peace" refers to an upright person, or one who follows after peace and the blessings of God.

JOHN 17:12
12 While I was with them in the world, I kept them in thy name: those that thou gavest me I have kept, and none of them is lost, but the SON OF PERDI- TION; that the scripture might be fulfilled.

JOHN 17:12 (*Weymouth, 3rd Edition*)
While I was with them, I kept them true to Thy name — the name Thou hast given me to bear — and I kept watch over them, and not one of them is lost but only he who is DOOMED TO DESTRUC- TION — that the scripture may be fulfilled.

Judas is called in this scripture the "son of perdition," or one deserving perdition.

EPHESIANS 2:3
3   Among whom also we all had our conversation in times past in the lusts of our flesh, fulfilling the desires of the flesh and of the mind; and were by nature the CHILDREN OF WRATH, even as others.

EPHESIANS 2:3 (*Weymouth, 3rd Edition*)
Among them all of us also formerly passed our lives, governed by the inclinations of our lower natures, indulging the cravings of those natures and of our own thoughts, and were in our original state DESERVING OF ANGER like all others.

We were the "children of wrath," meaning we were worthy of or deserved God's wrath.

A second example of an idiom of the Hebrew language is to show the greatness or excellence of a thing by using the words "of God" in connection with it. For instance:

ACTS 7:20
20 In which time Moses was born, and was
EXCEEDING FAIR, and nourished up in his
father's house three months.

In this verse, the *King James Version* paraphrases the idiom into a more modern expression, but in the original Greek, "exceeding fair" is actually "fair unto God." *Young's Literal Translation of the Holy Bible* gives us a more literal translation of the Greek.

ACTS 7:20 (*Young*)
In which time Moses was born, and he was FAIR
TO GOD, and he was brought up three months in
the house of his father.

Another example of this idiom can be seen in Psalm 80:10:

PSALM 80:10
10 The hills were covered with the shadow of it,
and the boughs thereof were like the GOODLY
CEDARS.

"Goodly cedars" is literally "cedars of God," as translated in Young:

PSALM 80:10 (*Young*)
Covered have been hills with its shadow, and its
boughs are CEDARS OF GOD.

JONAH 3:3
3 So Jonah arose, and went unto Nineveh,
according to the word of the Lord. Now Nineveh
was an EXCEEDING GREAT CITY of three days'
journey.

Here, "exceeding great city" is more literally "a great city of God." Once again, we see a more literal rendering in Young's translation:

JONAH 3:3
3   And Jonah riseth, and he goeth unto Nineveh,
according to the word of Jehovah. And Nineveh
hath been a GREAT CITY BEFORE GOD, a journey
of three days.

A third example of an idiom is used in order to emphasize
something. In this idiom, a word is doubled to show emphasis.
Notice:

2 CORINTHIANS 4:17
17 For our light affliction, which is but for a
moment, worketh for us a far more exceeding and
eternal WEIGHT OF GLORY.

"Weight of glory" signifies both weight and glory. Moffatt
gives us a more modern interpretation:

2 CORINTHIANS 4:17 (*Moffatt*)
The slight trouble of the passing hour results in a
SOLID GLORY PAST ALL COMPARISON.

EPHESIANS 1:19
19 And what is the exceeding greatness of his
power to usward who believe, according to the
working of his MIGHTY POWER.

Here, "might" and "power," two words meaning practically
the same thing, are used together to emphasize how mighty
and powerful God is.

Another example of a Hebraism can be seen in the expressions "to be found" or "to be called," which are often used to
show a state of being.

MATTHEW 1:18
18 Now the birth of Jesus Christ was on this wise:
When as his mother Mary was espoused to Joseph,
before they came together, SHE WAS FOUND
WITH CHILD of the Holy Ghost.

Principal (of Lynton Bible School, Devon, England) P. G. Parker gives us a more modern way of translating this idiom:

MATTHEW 1:18
18 Now the birth of Jesus Christ was in this way. His mother, Mary, was betrothed to Joseph, but as was the custom they did not live together during the first year, although regarded as man and wife. During this preliminary year Mary BECAME PREGNANT through the Holy Ghost.

More examples of this idiom expressing a state of being can be seen in the following scriptures:

HEBREWS 11:5
5   By faith Enoch was translated that he should not see death; and WAS NOT FOUND, because God had translated him: for before his translation he had this testimony, that he pleased God.

HEBREWS 11:5 (*Hudson*)
It was by faith that Enoch was removed [to heaven], so that he DID NOT SEE DEATH, and he was not overtaken by death [or, and he COULD NOT BE FOUND], because God took him to heaven. For before he was taken to heaven he obtained the record of having truly pleased God.

GENESIS 5:24
24 And Enoch walked with God: and HE WAS NOT; for God took him.

GENESIS 5:24 (*Young*)
And Enoch walketh habitually with God, AND HE IS NOT, for God hath taken him.

Notice that in Hebrews 11:5, Enoch was not found. This expression is translated "and he was not" in Genesis 5:24.

PHILIPPIANS 2:8
8   And BEING FOUND IN FASHION AS A MAN, he humbled himself, and became obedient unto death, even the death of the cross.

G. W. Wade gives us a picture of a modern-day equivalent
of this idiom:

PHILIPPIANS 2:8 (*G. W. Wade*)
Being, BY REASON OF SUCH OUTWARD
APPEARANCE, TAKEN TO BE ONLY MAN, He
humbled Himself further, and became submissive
to the Divine Will to the extent of enduring death,
yes, death on a Cross!

ISAIAH 9:6
6   For unto us a child is born, unto us a son is
given: and the government shall be upon his shoul-
der: AND HIS NAME SHALL BE CALLED
Wonderful, Counsellor, The mighty God, The ever-
lasting Father, The Prince of Peace.

Notice that Knox, in rendering it into modern language,
gives this idiom in the form of a question:

ISAIAH 9:6 (*Knox*)
For our sakes a child is born, to our race a son is
given, whose shoulder will bear the sceptre of
princely power. WHAT NAME SHALL BE GIVEN
HIM? Peerless among counsellors, the mighty God,
Father of the world to come, the Prince of peace.

The terms "loving" and "hating" are often used to show a
choosing of one thing over another. Notice that the modern
renderings of the following verses emphasize the preference of
one thing over another.

JOHN 12:25
25 He that LOVETH his life shall lose it; and he
that HATETH his life in this world shall keep it
unto life
eternal.

JOHN 12:25 (*Crofts*)
Whoever CLINGS to his physical life loses it, but
whoever is WILLING TO SACRIFICE HIS LIFE in
this world, will preserve it eternally.

LUKE 14:26
26 If any man come to me, and HATE not his father, and mother, and wife, and children, and brethren, and sisters, yea, and his own life also, he cannot be my disciple.

LUKE 14:26 (*Johnson*)
If any person encounters me and desires to be deeply related to me, HIS RELATIONSHIP TO ME MUST HAVE PRIORITY over his father, mother, wife, children, brothers, sisters, and his own safety. Unless it does, he cannot be my understudy.

ROMANS 9:13
13 As it is written, Jacob have I loved, but Esau have I HATED.

ROMANS 9:13 (*Richart*)
Elsewhere God states, "I PREFER JACOB TO ESAU."

Many such idioms abound in the *King James Version*. A very literal translation, such as *Young's Literal Translation of the Holy Bible*, is sure to abound in the idioms of the original language. Renderings into modern English, such as *Weymouth's, Moffatt's, Twentieth Century, New International Version* and others, have the least amount of these Hebraisms. Our own English idioms, if translated literally into Greek or Hebrew, would baffle those who know those languages but are not acquainted with ours. For this reason a strictly literal translation could be unintelligible to most English readers.

---

[1] *The CottonPatch Version of Paul's Epistles*
Chicago: Association Press, 1968.

Part III

The History of the Bible

Chapter 12
Early Bible History

Original Language of the Bible

Most of the Old Testament was originally written in Hebrew. The rest was written in Chaldee, sometimes referred to as Aramaic or Syriac. These Chaldee references are Ezra 4:8-6:18; 7:12-26; Daniel 2:4-7:28; Jeremiah 10:11, and two words, "Jegar-sahadutha," in Genesis 31:47 (a place meaning *heap of witnesses*).

All of the New Testament was written in Greek. (There is a theory that the Book of Matthew was originally written in Hebrew and then later translated into Greek, but we cannot be one hundred percent sure of that.) Except for the Book of Hebrews, the New Testament was basically written to Greek-speaking Gentiles. The Greek which was used to write the New Testament was called Koine, which was the common everyday language of its day. This Greek is somewhat different from other early Greek writings which were written in Classical Greek. In fact, the Greek text of New Testament times looks nothing like the Greek text found in today's writings.

John 1:1 from the original way of writing:

ΕΝΑΡΧΗΗΝΟΛΟΓΟΣΚΑΙΟΛΟΓΟΣΗΝΠΡΟΣΤΟΝΘΕΟΝ ΚΑΙΘΕΟΣΗΝΟΛΟΓΟΣ

Notice how all of the words are in capitals and run together without any spacing or punctuation markings.

Here is John 1:1 the way it is presented in today's Greek form:

Ἐν ἀρχῇ ἦν ὁ λόγος, καὶ ὁ λόγος ἦν πρὸς τὸν Θεόν, καὶ Θεὸς ἦν ὁ λόγος.

History of Modern Format

Chapter Divisions in the Old Testament

Chapter divisions in the Old Testament appear to have developed for the guidance of the reader in the synagogue. They were used to show the reader a suitable place at which he would begin and end his reading.

Chapter Divisions in the New Testament

The New Testament was divided into chapters soon after it was compiled. The first chapters were shorter than the ones that we use today. Modern chapter divisions are usually attributed to the Archbishop of Canterbury, Stephen Langton, who died in 1228. The first chapter divisions were made in the Latin Vulgate Bible shortly after 1200. They showed up in Wycliffe's (sometimes spelled "Wyclif") version of the New Testament in 1382, and have been retained in most subsequent English Versions since.

Verse Divisions in the Old Testament

Verse divisions in the Old Testament were introduced after the division of verses in the New Testament. The Jews arranged their Bible after the order found in the Christian Bible.

Verse Divisions in the New Testament

Verse divisions in the New Testament were first made by a French printer named Robert Estienne in 1551. He originally divided the verses to make a smaller unit of reference for a Greek concordance. Most of the work was done on horseback on a trip between Paris and Lyons. There were a total of 7,959 verses. These verse divisions first appeared in Estienne's fourth edition of the New Testament in Greek. It later became the standard to not only print the New Testament with these verse divisions, but also to print each verse as a paragraph.

Septuagint

The *Septuagint* is the oldest Greek translation of the Old Testament. It is sometimes referred to by the Roman numerals LXX, or seventy, because it was the work of seventy translators. Originally translated at Alexandria in the period of 275-100 B.C. by Hellenistic Jews, it was widely accepted at first by the Greek-speaking Jews.

After its adoption by the Christians, however, the Jews ceased to use it after about A.D. 70, not wanting to be found in connection in any way with the Christians. It is still used today by the Greek Orthodox Church. The *Septuagint* contains all the books of the Hebrew Bible. It was the Bible that both Jesus and the Apostle Paul quoted from. An unusual feature of the *Septuagint* is that it contained 151 Psalms. The 151st Psalm reads as follows from Thompson's translation of the *Septuagint*, which was the first Bible translated into English in America:

> **PSALM 151 (*Septuagint*)**
> **I was little among my brethren, and the youngest of my father's family. I fed my father's flocks. My hands had made an instrument and my fingers had tuned a psaltery. But who will tell my Lord? My Lord Himself heareth. He sent His messenger and took me from my father's flocks and anointed me with anointing oil. My brothers were comely and great; but the Lord did not delight in them. I went out to meet the Philistine, and he cursed me by his idols. But I drew his own sword and cut off his head, and took away reproach from the children of Israel.**

Latin Vulgate

It was during the second century A.D. that Latin first began to replace Greek as the dominant language of the Roman Empire. It was then that the need for a Latin Bible became apparent. There were a few translations of the Old Testament into Latin at that time, but these were not considered reliable, since they were translated from the Septuagint and not the original Hebrew. Since the New Testament was written originally in Greek, there were also a few translations of it as well, which were a little better accepted. But the need for one complete and authorized Bible to replace all these competing translations soon became apparent. It was then that Damasus, bishop of Rome (366-384), appointed his secretary, Jerome, to undertake this translation.

Jerome undertook the task with hesitation because he knew that some would take offense at his translation, no matter how good it was. He began with the Gospels, followed by the Psalms, and then translated the remainder of the New Testament. Jerome then had to master the Hebrew language in order to translate the Old Testament into Latin. He completed his translation in A.D. 405. Jerome's translation of the Bible is known as the Latin Vulgate.

It was not immediately accepted. Many rejected it because it was quite different from the version they were used to. But in time, because of its outstanding qualities, it became very popular. The Latin Vulgate is especially important because it was the first Bible to arrive in Western Europe, and it remained the accepted version in this part of the world for centuries. In fact, it was not until the twentieth century that any Bible translation besides the Latin Vulgate was recognized by the Roman Catholic Church.

Chapter 13
Early English Translations

All through time, people have wanted God's Word in a language they could understand. The earliest known portion of the Bible to be translated into English, or at least into the language of the Anglo-Saxon's, was Caedmon's rendering of the creation of the world, the nomadic movement of the children of Israel, and the story of Jesus. This was done during the seventh century and would not be called a translation, but rather a retelling of the accounts according to his everyday language.

Some of the copies of this work still exist today as well as some copies of the works of King Alfred. King Alfred's works include a portion of the Psalms which he made before his death in 901. A monk of Jarrow known as The Venerable Bede also made a translation of the Gospel of John from the Greek into his own everyday speech. History tells us that he had just finished dictating his work to younger monks when he died in May of 735.

The Book of Psalms seems to have been the most frequently translated (or paraphrased) book of Scripture, and has remained so through the years since. Many of the translations were done by writing the English translation between the lines of the older Latin manuscripts.

Our English Bible, regardless of the version, is only a translation from the original languages in which the Bible was written. All of the original documents disappeared long ago.

The English Bible has developed over many years and through the efforts of countless scholars. Over the years, literally hundreds of translations have been made. Currently, we see a new English version emerge nearly every year. Never have there been so many translations of the Scriptures available to read and study from.

The variety and types of these translations varies greatly, from very literal translations to loose paraphrases. The emergence of these new translations reflects the everchanging nature of the English language. The large number and variety of translations available, however, has recently caused some to wonder about the accuracy and value of modern translations. Many question whether the translator's personal doctrinal bias will affect the way he translates certain passages.

Unfortunately, translators don't always accurately capture the variant meanings of words when translating from the original text. No two languages correspond word for word. No translation, however scholarly, can do more than approximate the thought. Variant shades of meaning in the original language are difficult to maintain, and idioms are often hard to transfer. Translators may, even without meaning to, translate with a bias toward their own doctrinal beliefs.

What we must understand, however, is that although the Scriptures in their original writings were inspired by God, or God given, the translations are not. No translation will be perfect. But, keeping this in mind, let us not miss out on the value of Bible translations. Do not be afraid to use them, but rather learn to use them properly. Let one translation be a kind of commentary to another, adding richness and color to the meaning of the verse or passage.

Notice the following quote from Miles Coverdale, a Bible translator from the sixteenth century:

Now for thy part, most gentle reader, take in good worth that I here offer thee with a good will, and let this present translation be no prejudice to the other that out of the Greek have been translated afore, or shall be hereafter. For if thou open thine eyes and consider well the gift of the Holy Ghost therein, thou shalt see that one translation declareth, openeth and illustrateth another, and in many cases is a plain commentary unto another.[1]

John Wycliffe

John Wycliffe (sometimes spelled Wyclif, as we saw before), born approximately in 1320 near Richmond in Yorkshire, England, is best remembered as a church reformer and Bible translator. He spent most of his adult life at Oxford University, where he was a teacher of theology. Wycliffe became known as a brilliant scholastic theologian and the most respected debater of his time. Wycliffe spoke out against the church of his day, calling for a reformation of its wealth, corruption, and abuses. He rejected the Biblical basis of papal authority and advocated radical church reform. He also advocated the translation of the Bible into English for the public, rather than the Latin version of his day, which most could not read. Stemming from this belief, Wycliffe supervised an English translation of the Bible. (The actual work was done by his understudies.)

It was his views on this and other matters that caused his writings to be condemned by the church. Sometime during the year of 1374 he was made rector of Lutterworth, and it was here that he remained until his death near the end of 1384. Wycliffe himself was never tried nor personally condemned during his lifetime, but thirty-one years after his death, his body was exhumed by the church and burned.

The Wycliffe New Testament was first issued in 1380, and later revised by his secretary, John Purvey. The following are examples from these two editions:

EPHESIANS 1:12 (*Wycliffe 1380 Edition*)
Poul the apostel of ihesus crist, bi the wille of god, to alle seyntis that ben at effecie, and to the feithful men in ihesus crist.

EPHESIANS 1:12 (*Wycliffe 1388 Edition*)
Poul, the apostle of Jhesu Crist, bi the wille of God, to alle seyntis that ben at Effesis, and to the feithful men in Jhesu Crist.

The spelling may look a little strange to you, but remember that these versions were made a good hundred years before Columbus landed in America.

Theodore Beza

Theodore Beza was a French theologian, born June 24, 1519, and died October 13, 1605. He succeeded John Calvin as the leader of Reformed Protestantism. Beza was the most noted Biblical scholar of his time and published a critical edition of the Greek New Testament in 1565, based on seventeen Greek manuscripts. Its influence can be seen in most if not all of the Bible translations from the Geneva Bible to the *King James Version*.

William Tyndale

William Tyndale was born around 1494, in Gloucestershire, England. He was one of the early English Protestant reformers, but he is best known for his English translation of the Bible. He was educated at Oxford and Cambridge.

It was William Tyndale who made the statement to one of the leaders of the church, *If God spare my life, ere many years I will cause a boy that driveth the plough shall know more of the Scripture than thou dost.* Later in his life he wrote these words, *I had perceaved by experyence, how that it was impossible to stablysh the laye people in any truth, excepte the scripture were playnly layde before their eyes in their mother tonge, that they might see the processes ordre and meaninge of the text.*

In 1524, after failing to find sponsorship in England for his translation, he moved to Germany. When copies of his New Testament arrived in England the work was attacked by the church regime, who petitioned for his death as a heretic. Tyndale lived most of his life away from England after that. He was also known to write Protestant tracts.

Tyndale's writings show the influence of Martin Luther, with whom he became acquainted while in Germany. In fact, it was Luther who was probably responsible for his conversion to Protestantism. Unlike earlier English translators, Tyndale was a master of Greek and Hebrew terms. Tyndale's 1534 version was the principle source for the *King James* and later versions.

In 1535 he was arrested and imprisoned at Vilvorde, near Brussels. He was condemned for heresy and executed. When he was martyred on October 6,1536, he prayed that the eyes of the king would be opened to the need for the common people to have the Word of God. This prayer was answered a little over a year after his death.

George Joye

George Joye's New Testament, printed in 1534, was, for the most part, simply a copy of Tyndale's New Testament with a few changes. There is only one known copy in existence. William Tyndale protested firmly against this adaptation of his New Testament, which was done without his authorization.

He especially disliked the use of the phrase "life after this life," which Joye inserted in place of the word "resurrection." But Tyndale's major objection was the fact that Joye did not even bother to put his own name on the work, but left Tyndale's name on it.

Miles Coverdale

Miles Coverdale, born sometime in 1488, died January 20, 1569. He is honored with having published the first complete English Bible. Like Tyndale, he was a graduate of Cambridge but never attended Oxford. He was not the scholar that his friend William Tyndale was, but according to *Foxe's Book of English Martyrs* he helped Tyndale work on sections of the Old Testament.

It was, in fact, Tyndale's translation of the New Testament that Coverdale used as a basis for his own work. He also consulted some foreign versions while working on his version. This practice of consulting previous versions was later used by the translators of the *King James Version* of the Bible. Coverdale was the first one to place chapter summaries in the Bible. He also was the first to remove the Apocryphal books from the Old Testament and place them in a separate section. This practice has been followed by all Protestant Bibles ever since (that is, the ones that have included the Apocrypha).

We still find some of the flavor of the Coverdale Bible in the *King James Version*. A good example can be seen in Matthew 25:21. Looking first at the Tyndale version we will begin to see how some of the early translators would follow the work that was done before them and use the same terms in their own renderings. Some would prefer the wording of the master linguist William Tyndale (he could read and speak more than a dozen languages), yet others would choose to use the more eloquent phrase of Miles Coverdale.

> MATTHEW 25:21 (*Tyndale 1535*)
> Then his master sayde unto him: well good servaunt and faythfull. Thou hast bene faythfull in lytell, I will make the ruler over moche: entre in into thy masters joye.

> MATTHEW 25:21 (*Tyndale Modem Spelling*)
> Then his master said unto him: well good servant and faithful. Thou hast been faithful in little, I will make thee ruler over much: enter in into thy master's joy.

> MATTHEW 25:21
> 21 His lord said unto him, Well done, thou good and f aithf ul servant: thou hast been f aithf ul over a few things, I will make thee ruler over many things: enter thou into the joy of thy lord.

It is from the work of Coverdale that we get the phrase *"enter thou into the joy of the Lord."* This is a phrase that we all feel at home with and occasionally use in reference to our relationship with the Lord. Other translators used this phrase as well in their own works, including the Great Bible, the Bishop's Bible and even the Catholic Rheims New Testament. The Geneva Bible chose to retain Tyndale's choice of words and the newer *Revised Standard Version* of 1946 also went back to the rendering of Tyndale.

Coverdale also worked on the Great Bible two years after his own was published. He often came to prefer the renderings of the other versions he helped with over his own.

Thomas Matthew

The name Thomas Matthew was an alias for a man named John Rogers, who was born around 1500. He was educated at Cambridge, earning a B.A. degree in 1525. He also was a friend of William Tyndale. The title page of the Bible he compiled bears the name of Thomas Matthew, but it was well known to be the work of John Rogers. Even during his trial under the reign of Queen Mary he was referred to as "John Rogers, alias Matthew." His is a very interesting version of the Bible, in that for the most part it is still the work of William Tyndale. In the Old Testament we find Tyndale's original translation of the Pentateuch (the first five books of the Old Testament) with very few changes. Then from the Book of Joshua to the Second Book of Chronicles, the translation used, according to tradition and to the style of writing, is the unpublished work of Tyndale which he made while in prison awaiting his execution.

The remainder of the Old Testament, Ezra to Malachi and the Apocrypha, is the work of Miles Coverdale. Then, turning to the New Testament we find Tyndale's last revision which he made in 1535, with only a few changes. One of the most outstanding changes we do find in this version is his translation of the word "Hallelujah," which he renders "Praise the everlasting."

The magnitude of this Bible is that it put together all of William Tyndale's work with Miles Coverdale's version making up the rest. In fact, sixty-five percent of the whole Bible was the work of William Tyndale, which later proved to be the basis for the Bishop's Bible, the Great Bible, and the King James version with its revisions. John Rogers was martyred in February, 1555. He was the first to be martyred under the reign of Mary Stuart, Queen of the Scots.

Richard Taverner

Richard Taverner was born around 1505. He was educated at both Cambridge and Oxford. While he was at Oxford he was imprisoned just for reading a William Tyndale New Testament. After his release he was imprisoned once again in the infamous Tower of London for working on an English translation of the Bible. He was released again and later even became the high sheriff of the county of Oxford.

Taverner's text is basically that of Matthew's Bible, however, he did make some alterations in the text. The Old Testament echoes the influence of the Latin Vulgate. Because he was accomplished as a Greek scholar, the New Testament shows more changes, as he also followed closely the text of William Tyndale. We owe such phrases found in the *King James Version* as "parable" and "Passover" to Richard Taverner. He died in 1575.

Edmund Becke

This Bible is sometimes called *Bishop Becke's Bible*. It was, for the most part, the text of Taverner's translation in the Old Testament and that of Tyndale's in the New Testament. He did, however, add a translation of Third Maccabees and retranslate the Apocryphal books of First Esdras, Tobit, and Judith. He was ahead of his time in his preface, in which he dedicated his translation to the king, and exhorted the king to godly living as an example to his subjects.

Becke said that if the people of his day would spend only one hour a day reading the Bible that they would in turn *give up gambling and vices that tend toward an unholy life*. One annotation, however, which I find very questionable is his note on First Peter 3:7, which reads as follows:

*He dwelleth with his wife according to knowledge,
that taketh her as a necessary helper, and not as a
bond servant, or a bond slave. And if she be not obedient and helpful unto him, endeavoureth to beat the fear
of God into her head, that thereby she may be com-
pelled to learn her duties and to do it.*

The Great Bible

The Great Bible, released in 1538 by permission of King
Henry VIII, was so called because of its great size. During the
years of 1525-1526, William Tyndale's Bibles were publicly
burned and the only English Bibles at that time were the *The
Thomas Matthew Bible* and the *Coverdale Bible*. These,
however, were full of various notes by the translators which
the church authorities did not look favorably upon. Thus King
Henry VIII authorized Cromwell to make arrangements for a
new English Bible. Miles Coverdale was appointed as the main
editor. Copies of this Bible were chained to the pulpit in the
churches so that the common people could come and read
them.

Most of the people could not read, however, so certain days
were set aside for public reading (the Bible was read from the
Latin during church services). On this day, multitudes would
show up to hear the Word of God being read in English. Much
of William Tyndale's influence is seen in the Great Bible.

Geneva Bible

It was during the reign of Mary, Queen of Scots, ("Bloody
Mary," as she is known in history) that the Protestant reformers began gathering in Geneva, Switzerland. It was there that
William Whittingham, a brother-in-law of John Calvin,
revised the New Testament of the Great Bible. This was first

printed in 1557, and was the first English version to divide the chapters into verses. It also italicized all the English words which have no corresponding words in the Greek.

This New Testament had an abundance of notes as well as long chapter summaries. A little over two years later the full Bible was printed. It was revised and printed many times after that. In fact, according to the American Bible Society, from 1560 to 1644 one hundred forty editions of the Bible and Testament in this version were issued. This version of the Bible became very popular with the common people who spoke English. It was the Bible that came over on the Mayflower, the Bible that Shakespeare used, and the Bible of John Bunyon (the writer of *Pilgrim's Progress*).

The Bishop's Bible

Even though the Geneva Bible was superior to the Great Bible, and was widely accepted by the majority of the people, it was never sanctioned as the authorized Bible of the church. After all, the Geneva Bible was the Bible of the Puritans, and by now a great faction had grown between the state church and the Puritans, who represented the way the common people wanted to worship the Lord.

In 1559, Queen Elizabeth appointed Matthew Parker as Archbishop of Canterbury. He was a man of authentic virtue and blameless morals, but unfortunately, he just could not accept the freedom of the Puritans.

Parker began the work on a new Bible to be authorized by the church. He divided the work among a group of scholars with at least eight of them being bishops. The remainder later became bishops. Hence the name, The Bishop's Bible. Parker was the one who did the final editing, as well as revising Genesis, Exodus, and certain sections of the New Testament.

The basis of this new revision was the Great Bible. And because the revisers were better Greek scholars than they were with the Hebrew language, the New Testament is by far better than the Old. In fact, the Old Testament shows influence from the Geneva Bible, which is the very one that the church wanted to stay away from. There were a number of fresh changes made in the New Testament straight from the Greek text, which was then available to them. Some of these later showed up in the *King James Version* of the Bible. The Bishop's Bible was first printed in 1568, and continued to be the Bible found in the churches of England until the *King James Version* replaced it. There were no editions printed after 1602.

It is interesting to note that during one of the revisions of this Bible the text of the Psalms was replaced with that of the former version of the Great Bible. This was because the Psalter of the Prayer Book used during public worship was that of the Great Bible, and they thought it was awkward to have two versions of the Psalms used in the church. (This Psalter was used in the Prayer Book up until the middle part of this century.) The Bishop's Bible was the second Bible to be authorized by the church.

The Douay-Rheims Bible

There are four translations of the Bible still in use today that are older than the *King James Version*. These are the Septuagint, which, as we saw, is a Greek translation of the Hebrew Bible (Old Testament); Jerome's Latin Vulgate, which is a translation out of the original languages; Martin Luther's German Bible; and the Douay-Rheims. All of these Bibles can still be bought and used today, although the Douay-Rheims Bible has undergone major revisions since it was first published. It is a Catholic Bible, which is named, like the Geneva

Bible, after a town (two towns) rather than some person or group. The Old Testament, which was translated first but printed last was done at the English college at Douay.

The New Testament was done at Rheims while the college was located there for a while before moving back to Douay. This is why sometimes the whole Bible is referred to as the Douay Bible and the New Testament is called the Rheims New Testament. The New Testament was printed in 1582. It was consulted by the *King James* translators. The Old Testament was printed in 1610, too late for the *King James* translators to use. It was primarily the work of Gregory Martin as translator, with a few others adding the annotations. Unlike the *King James Version*, it was a fresh translation. It makes a good study Bible in that it translates the idioms straight across, which means that the thought of the idiom is translated from one language to the next, rather than being an exact word-for-word translation.

The King James Version

King James VI of Scotland became King James I of England in 1604. Shortly thereafter, he authorized the first Protestant Bible. It was, in fact, Dr. John Reynolds, a Puritan spokesman, who first suggested that a new translation be made. To see the irony of this translation, one needs only to realize that Mary, Queen of Scots, the same Queen Mary known for her determination to stamp out Protestantism by burning Protestants at the stake, was his mother. (She takes up a considerable amount of space in *Foxe's Book of English Martyrs.*) That her son is the one whose name is attached to the most beloved Bible of all time is somewhat of a parody.

The *King James Bible* was printed early in 1611. The first edition was often called the *He Bible* because of the way that it translated Ruth 3:15: ". . . he went into the city," instead of the way that it is now rendered in the *King James Bible*: ". . . *she went into the city.*" The different copies of the *King James Bible* between 1611 and 1614 had either he or she, then it was finally settled to use "she." The *King James Bible* underwent major revisions in 1615, 1629, 1638, and in 1762. It was not until forty years after it was printed that it became the accepted Bible of the people, and even though it claims to be the *Authorized Version*, it was the third such Bible to make this claim. Some today believe that the *King James Version* is the only "inspired" version of the Bible, but through all of its beauty and prose, it is still just a translation. Much of it, in fact, is still the work of William Tyndale. Quoting from the pen of Edgar Goodspeed:[2]

> *It is, in fact, in the New Testament at least, no more than a revision of his (Tyndale's) final edition of 1535, being a revision of the Bishops', which was a revision of the Great Bible, which was in turn a revision of John Rogers', which embodied the last work of Tyndale. It is not too much to say that William Tyndale wrote nine-tenths of the King James New Testament.*

Through all of the revisions that it has undergone there is still a misprint that has been left untouched for so long that it has become a part of the *King James Bible*. In Matthew 23:24 we find: "*Ye blind guides, which strain AT a gnat, and swallow a camel.*" This should be rendered, "*strain OUT a gnat.*"

We can also look back and notice some of the more interesting mistakes that were corrected. In the first edition in Mark 10:18 it read: "*And Jesus said unto him, Why callest thou me good? there is NO MAN good but one, that is, God.*"

Which was later changed to: "*And Jesus said unto him, Why callest thou me good? there is NONE good but one, that is, God.*"

Then there was the infamous *Wicked Bible* printed in 1631 which left out the word "not" in Exodus 20:14 making it read, "Thou shalt commit adultery." The printer was given a heavy fine of 300 pounds. In 1717 there was an edition known as the *Vingar Bible* which used the word "vingar" in the heading for the Parable of the Vineyard. It read "The Parable of the Vingar." There was even a *Murderer's Bible* printed in 1795 which read, *"But Jesus said unto her, Let the children first be KILLED: for it is not meet to take the children's bread, and to cast* [it] *unto the dogs"* (Mark 7:27). Of course it should have read, *". . . Let the children first be FILLED."*

In 1802, a Bible was printed in which First Timothy 5:21 read, *"I DISCHARGE thee before God."* It should have read, *"I CHARGE thee before God."*

In 1829, one printing had in Isaiah 66:9, *"Shall I bring to the birth, and not CEASE to bring forth?"* This should have been, *"Shall I bring to the birth, and not CAUSE to bring forth?"*

In Psalm 14:1, one edition had, *"The fool hath said in his heart, 'There is A God.'"* Of course, it should have read, *"The fool hath said in his heart, 'There is NO God.'"*

In Second Samuel 23:20 we had, *"And Benaiah the son of Jehoiada, the son of a valiant man, of Kabzeel, who had done many acts, he slew TWO LIONS LIKE MEN of Moab: he went down also and slew a lion in the midst of a pit in time of snow."* This should have read: *"And Benaiah the son of Jehoiada, the son of a valiant man, of Kabzeel, who had done many acts, he slew TWO LIONLIKE MEN of Moab: he went down also and slew a lion in the midst of a pit in time of snow."*

Finally, we can see the humor of all this in this outstanding mistake found in Psalm 119:161, for instead of reading, *"PRINCES have persecuted me without a cause: but my heart standeth in awe of thy word,"* some unfortunate printer's work must have gotten the best of him for we *read, "PRINTERS have persecuted me without a cause: but my heart standeth in awe of thy word."*

[1] Curtis Vaughan, gen. ed., *The New Testament from 26 Translations* (Grand Rapids: Zondervan, 1967).

[2] Edgar J. Goodspeed, *The Making of the English New Testament* (Chicago: The University of Chicago Press, 1925) p. 51.

Chapter 14
Translations After 1611

There have been many, many translations made since 1611, some which are hard to tell apart from the *King James Version* itself, and others that are nothing like the *King James Version* at all. These range from very literal translations to blown out paraphrases. Some of the paraphrases, in fact, are so freely rendered that one questions where the paraphraser came up with it. For the most part, however, I have found that the translators and paraphrasers have been honest in their dealing with the Word of God. There are, however, exceptions to this rule, the most infamous of these being the *New World Translation of the Holy Scriptures* published by the Jehovah Witnesses. Here we find that the translation is made to fit their doctrine, and not the other way around.

There are others also who have an ax to grind and are looking for a soapbox from which to make their devilish claims. These I highly recommend that you stay away from. These types of translations are, fortunately, few and far between. It does help to know what the translators believed and taught, but remember, no one translation can ever be without fault.

There are many ways in which you can use your Bible translations. You may choose to use certain ones for devotional readings like *The Living Bible* or *Good News For Modern Man*. Paraphrases and modern language Bibles are good for that sort of reading. They can be used to help you better understand what you have read from the version you usually use. Listed below are some of the versions that you may want to use. Some you can buy right off the shelf at a local bookstore. Others may not be so readily available to you, but you most likely will run across references to them in some of the books that you read or will hear them quoted from by various ministers.

This information is given to help acquaint you with the various translations that have been made. I have kept this list short, as this is not the purpose of this book. You may wish to learn more about the various translations of the Bible. If so, there are many good books on this subject that go into much more detail than I have at this point.

1755 John Wesley

John Wesley's New Testament is actually a revision of the *King James Version*. Even back then, John Wesley felt that the language of the *King James Bible* was too archaic and set out to bring it up to date. It is best known for the notes that are found in it. It is, in fact, called *Explanatory Notes Upon The New Testament*. It is worth getting for these notes as they are useful both for outlining a godly life and explanations of many texts. He gives some interesting renderings, such as this one found in First Corinthians:

> **1 CORINTHIANS 14:15**
> **15 What then is my duty? I will pray with the spirit, but I will pray with understanding also: I will sing with the spirit, but I will sing with the understanding also.**

1876 Julia Smith

Julia Smith has the distinct honor of being the first woman to have translated the Bible. She was well into her later years when she made the meritorious feat. One of the most outstanding features of her Bible is that she had to learn Greek and Hebrew before she could begin. This was a very remarkable feat for someone in her golden years.

Since she was the first woman to have made a translation, this has become one of the most sought after Bibles for Bible collectors. As far as I can tell, it was only printed once. She had some unusual renderings — First John 3:8 for instance. The *King James* says:

> **1 JOHN 3:8**
> **8   He that committeth sin is of the devil; for the devil sinneth from the beginning. For this purpose the Son of God was manifested, that he might destroy the works of the devil.**

She rendered the last part of the verse as ". . . unemploy the devil."

1881-1885 English Revised Version

The *Revised Version* came into being as the result of a need for a more accurate version of the Bible to be made available. It was immediately widely accepted and sales of the new translation were very high. People were ready for an updated version of the Bible. In fact, the need for a new translation was so great that when the *Revised Version of the New Testament* was released in New York on a Friday, which was the day that it was released in London, publishers in Chicago, not wanting to wait the twenty-six hours it would take to get the Bible from New York by train, sent a team of ninety operators to New York who telegraphed the whole New Testament — Matthew to Revelation — back to Chicago. This way they were able to put it into print and have it ready to sell on Saturday.

1899 Twentieth Century New Testament — Tentative Edition

The Twentieth Century New Testament was one of the early pioneers of modern speech Bibles that seemed to pave the way for the ones to come. Although there were others that had been done before this, *The Twentieth Century New Testament* was more of a stage-setter than the others. It is very similar to the one that was printed as the *New Testament in Modern Speech* by Dr. Richard Weymouth a few years later. Dr. Weymouth, in fact, played a small part in the development of this New Testament.

This translation was the work of twenty translators who never once met together, but corresponded by mail. They later added another twelve translators to the team, but we know nothing of them. Of the original twenty we find a wide range of individuals who took part in producing a New Testament that was modern and that young people could understand. Their ages ranged from nineteen to past sixty. Almost half of them were ministers or retired ministers. They came from many different denominations and were concerned only with producing a New Testament that was readable.

The tentative edition was to be released in two parts, the first being the four Gospels and the Book of Acts, and the second volume was to be the remainder of the New Testament. The overwhelming demand for such a translation was so large that they went ahead and released the bulk of Paul's letters in the second volume with volume three containing the Pastoral Letters, Philemon, and Hebrews. It also included the General Letters and Revelation.

The arrangement of the books in the New Testament are not what most of us are used to, as is the case with many translations. In fact, the arrangement of the books differs between the Tentative Edition and the Revised Edition.

In 1904 the *Twentieth Century New Testament — Revised Edition* was released. The note from the treasurer of the *Twentieth Century New Testament* shows us the results of issuing their New Testament as tentative. It reads:

"The 'Tentative Edition' of this Translation was issued in three parts between 1898 and 1901. In that Edition we endeavored to discover what was practicable in a modern translation of the New Testament, before issuing a permanent edition. This Revision of our Translation, rendered necessary by the large demand for our 'Tentative Edition' in every part of the English- speaking world, amounts practically to a careful retranslation made in the light of experience derived from our previous attempts, and of the many valuable criticisms that have been received."

1901 *American Standard Version*

This version of the Bible is basically the same as the *Revised Version* of 1881, except it inserted the renderings suggested by the American committee. They had to wait ten years before they could release this version.

1901 Moffatt's *Historical New Testament*

This little known version of the New Testament should not be confused with Moffatt's regular Bible. This one is a completely different translation, which he made for his doctorate degree. The title page reads: "The Historical New Testament Being The Literature Of The New Testament Arranged In The Order Of Its Literary Growth And According To The Dates Of The Documents. A New Translation Edited With Prolegomena, Historical Tables, Critical Notes, And An Appendix by James Moffatt, B.D." Moffatt also worked on the *Revised Standard Version*.

A story was once told to me about Moffatt's involvement with the *Revised Standard Version*. Apparently, a colleague submitted a particular rendering and it was turned down by

Moffatt. His coworker turned to him and said that what he had submitted was right out of Moffatt's very own translation, to which Moffatt replied that the rendering was okay for that translation but was unsuitable for the *Revised Standard Version*.

1903 Weymouth's *New Testament in Modern Speech*

This much loved translation has undergone six different editions and almost countless printings. It was the first private translation to sell over a million copies. But Dr. Richard Weymouth never lived long enough to see the fruit of his labors. In fact, he died before it ever went to press. The first three editions were edited and partly revised by Weymouth's friend Ernest Hampden-Cook. He made changes in each of the three that he worked on. (Although the second edition claims to be a revision of the first edition, I have found no changes whatsoever.)

The fourth edition was "newly revised by several well-known New Testament scholars." Then the fifth edition was edited by James Alexander Robertson. The sixth edition oddly enough has no other name but that of Weymouth, at least that I have ever seen. Close examination, however, shows that it is a fifth edition Weymouth with very few changes.

1913 Moffatt's Translation

James Moffatt was another of the modern language Bible translators. His New Testament was issued in 1913, followed by the Old Testament which was released in two volumes in 1924 and 1925. There were at least seventy printings of the Moffatt New Testament and full Bible between World War I and World War II. In fact, during that time period, when someone mentioned the "New Translation," this was the version they most likely meant. There are a few draw backs to this translation, one being that Moffatt considered himself a "modernist," or what we would call a liberal today.

Fortunately this really does not show up too much in his translation. The rearrangement of the location of whole passages without warning, however, tends to hinder rather than help the reader. It contains an excellent rendering of Paul's letters. In the Old Testament he always translates *Jehovah as the Eternal*.

1923 *The Bible: An American Translation, (Smith-Goodspeed)*

Edgar Goodspeed submitted a paper on translations of the New Testament to the New Testament Club of the University of Chicago in February of 1920. This eventually resulted in his translation of the New Testament. It has been claimed to be the best modern speech version ever produced in America. Statements like this are always open opinion, but, it has proved to be one of the best single author translations made in modern times. He used the Greek text of Westcott and Hort for the most part, but you can find where he departed from it in examples like:

1 PETER 3:19
19 By which also he went and preached unto the spirits in prison.

1 PETER 3:19 (*Goodspeed*)
In it ENOCH went and preached even to those spirits that were in prison.

JOHN 19:29
29 Now there was set a vessel full of vinegar: and they filled a sponge with vinegar, and put it upon hyssop, and put it to his mouth.

JOHN 19:29 (*Goodspeed*)
**A bowl of sour wine was standing there. So they
put a sponge soaked in the wine ON A PIKE and
held it to his lips.**

He abstained from such words as "thee," "thou," and "ye."
He wished to make his version as American as possible, and
even called it the *American Translation*. In 1931 Goodspeed's
New Testament was joined with the Old Testament edited by
J. M. Powis Smith and was called *The Bible: An American
Translation*.

There were some changes made when these two were combined, mostly in the Old Testament section. Later, in 1938,
Goodspeed made a translation of the Apocrypha which was
added to the Bible the following year. It was then called *The
Complete Bible: An American Translation*. Since then, it has
been printed both with the Apocrypha and without. The New
Testament section of this translation came out in twenty-five
daily newspapers. This shows us the hunger of people to have
the Bible in a language that they could understand.

1937 Charles B. Williams New Testament

The main feature of this New Testament produced by C. B.
Williams is its unique ability to enable English readers of the
New Testament to understand the various shades of the tenses
of Greek verbs. (I was considering listing it with the "translations as study Bibles" section because of this.) By taking a little
time and learning the meanings of a few verb types, which can
be done by reading through a good Greek grammar book, you
will be able to see what he has done with this translation. Of
course, you do not have to do this in order to benefit from this
version of the New Testament. A couple of quotes from an earlier edition will shed some light on the value of this translation:

Publisher's Preface

> *In the present volume the translator seeks to avoid
> . . . extremes. He adheres faithfully to the sense of the*

Greek, as well as rendering it into language easily understood by the average reader.

Foreword

This is not a word-for-word translation, like an interlinear. It is rather a translation of the thought of the writers with a reproduction of their diction and style. Greek idioms are not brought over into our translation, but are expressed in corresponding English idioms which express the same thoughts as the Greek idioms. It is the thoughts of our New Testament, not its single words, that we have tried to translate.

1946-1952 Revised Standard Version

This version of the Bible is a modern-day updating of the older *American Standard Version*. It is not as literal as the older *ASV*, being a more modern language version. Still, it retains the flavor of *Tyndale / King James Version*, which most other modern Bibles do not.

The work on this version began in 1937 by the International Council of Religious Education. There were some major changes made between the first edition of 1946 and the later edition of 1952. For example, the word "consecrate" used in the first edition was replaced by the word "sanctify" in the later edition. Two famous translators worked on the *RSV*, Edgar J. Goodspeed from America and James Moffatt from Scotland.

1958 *New Testament in Modern English* By J. B. Phillips

This modern language New Testament has been said by many to be the best version of its kind. It even replaced

Weymouth's New Testament in many publications on recommended books for students to get. Phillips never meant for his version to be printed. He originally made it for young people who were under his supervision during World War II.

After trying to read to them from the *King James Version* he found that they could not understand it. He then set out to make a translation they could understand. It would have never been published if it had not been for C. S. Lewis. It was Lewis' persuasion that finally convinced Phillips to publish *Letters To Young Churches* in 1947. In 1952, the *Gospels in Modern English* first appeared, to be followed by *The Young Church in Action* (Acts) in 1955 with the remainder of the New Testament released in 1957 under the title *The Book of Revelation*. The next year the New Testament was released in its entirety. This version was then revised in 1973.

The second edition is not quite as colorful a rendering as the first edition. If you only get one version of the Phillips, I recommend that you try to get the first edition, which can be readily found in many used bookstores. You may also prefer the student's edition, since it has the verse numbers in the margin, as opposed to the regular edition, which only occasionally gives the verse number. The student's edition is also much better for comparison study.

1971 *New American Standard*

The *New American Standard Bible* was the work of fifty-eight anonymous conservative Protestant scholars. The New Testament was first released in 1963 and the Old Testament in 1971. This translation was well received among evangelical Christians in America, but not very well received outside of the United States and evangelical circles. It is, overall, a very conservative and literal translation which seeks to give an accurate literal rendering of the Hebrew and Greek texts. It contains a good cross reference, notes, and other reader helps, which make it a good study Bible.

1961 Wuest's Expanded Translation

Wuest's *The New Testament: An Expanded Translation* originally came out in three volumes: the Gospels in 1956, Acts through Ephesians in 1958, and Philippians through Revelation in 1959. The entire New Testament in one volume came out in 1961. Wuest's translation follows the Greek order of words in a sentence, but is expanded to show emphasis and bring out subtle nuances and word meanings of the original Greek.

For instance, in Matthew 16:23, where the Lord says, *"Get thee behind me, Satan" (KJV)*, Wuest renders it, *"Be gone under my authority, and keep on going, behind me, out of my sight, Satan."* Another good example can be found in Hebrews 13:5, *"Let your conversation be without covetousness; and be content with such things as ye have: for he hath said, I will never leave thee, nor forsake thee" (KJV)*. Wuest translated this, *"Let your manner of life be without love of money, being satisfied with your present circumstances. For he himself has said, and the statement is on record, I will not, I will not cease to sustain and uphold you. I will not, I will not, I will not let you down."*

1965 *Amplified Bible*

The Amplified Bible was primarily the work of a woman, Frances E. Cerate, who, along with about a dozen other translators, sought to make a translation that would convey the whole thought of the original Greek or Hebrew text in an understandable format. In order to accomplish this, key words are "amplified" throughout the text. This amplification includes supplying synonyms and explanations for those key words which bring out shades of meaning that could not be seen in a word-for-word translation.

The amplifications are signified by dashes and parentheses. Brackets indicate cross references and words that are included for clarification, and italics indicate supplied conjunctions. This "amplified" approach can be very helpful for personal study. The broken up style of the text, however, can make it difficult for Bible reading.

1966 *Today's English Version* or *Good News for Modem Man*

The New Testament of the *Today's English Version Bible* was the work of one man, Robert G. Bratcher, a scholar in New Testament studies who had done translation work as a missionary in Brazil. He began the project of making a new translation at the request of the American Bible Society in 1964. A committee of six other scholars was later appointed to translate the Old Testament as well.

The *TEV* is overall a very accurate translation of the Greek and Hebrew in very easy-to-understand and contemporary language. Its common language is especially appropriate for new believers, children, and those with a limited vocabulary. It includes a section that defines words such as "amen" and "tithe" which were kept in the text but of which many readers may not know the meaning. There are four editions of the New Testament with changes found in each edition. Some of them are substantial. There is, however, only one version of the Old Testament.

1971 *Living Bible*

The Living Bible, a popular contemporary English paraphrase, was the result of Dr. Kenneth Taylor's attempt to paraphrase the Bible for his children to be used in family devotions. The first copies of the New Testament letters, entitled "Living

Letters," were published by Dr. Taylor in 1962. It was not until an endorsement by Billy Graham in 1963 that the paraphrase became popular. The complete New Testament was published in 1967 and the whole Bible in 1971.

On the whole, *The Living Bible* is very readable and interesting. *The Living Bible* is very good for reading or for family devotions, especially in the Old Testament and the Gospels.

1973 *Translator's New Testament*

Produced and printed by the British and Foreign Bible Society, the *Translator's New Testament* was made for the purpose of assisting missionaries doing translating work who do not know Greek and need to use the English to work from. It has several pages of translational notes and a good glossary in the back that help the translator. Since it is designed in this format, I have found it to be an excellent study Bible.

1978, *Holy Bible, New International Version*

The idea for a new contemporary English version was first endorsed by a large number of evangelical leaders, all from various denominational backgrounds, in 1966. Work on the translation began in 1967 with contributions from over 110 Bible scholars from the United States, Great Britain, Ireland, Canada, New Zealand, and Australia, all with varying denominational affiliation. The New Testament was released in 1973. When the full Bible was released in 1978, it sold over one million copies in its first printing.

This was the largest first printing of a Bible in history. Although it is traditional in much of its vocabulary, the *New International Version* replaces archaic pronouns and verbal inflections. It is written on a seventh-grade level, making it easy to read.

Part IV

Study Helps

Chapter 15
Brief Survey of the New Testament

Matthew: Sovereignty, (Behold the King). Keywords: Son of man, Son of God. Written for the Jews who knew the Old Testament. He records Israel's attitude toward Jesus as Messiah.

Mark: Ministry, (Behold My Servant). Keyword: Immediately. Written for the Romans.

Luke: Humanity, (Behold the Man). Keywords: Prayer, Repentance. Written to the Gentiles.

John: Deity, (Behold your God). Keyword: Eternal Life. Written to the Church.

Acts: A record of the Holy Spirit in the lives of the believers, primarily Peter and Paul.

Romans: Righteousness revealed; sanctification realized through the believer's identification with Christ.

First Corinthians: Church conduct and order; our union to each other in the Body of Christ.

Second Corinthians: The ministry of the believer; victorious Christian living.

Galatians: Grace verses law; the work of the Spirit in the life of those who have accepted Christ; a brief look into the life of Paul; flesh and spirit contrasted.

Ephesians: The believer is seated with Christ; the believer's walk in Christ; the believer exhorted to stand in the authority of Christ.

Philippians: A missionary letter; the believer's joy in Christ.

Colossians: Jesus Christ and His union with the church.

First Thessalonians: The rapture of the church; knowing those who labor among you.

Second Thessalonians: Christ's returning with His saints.

First Timothy: Church order and leadership.

Second Timothy: The pastoral ministry; instructions to the ministry.

Titus: Responsibility and church order.

Philemon: Christian love.

Hebrews: The better covenant; Jesus is the High Priest.

James: The perception of Christianity; the Proverbs of the New Testament.

First Peter: Salvation, submission, and suffering in the life of the believer; Christ is the only hope.

Second Peter: Development of Christian virtues; the end times.

First John: Eternal life and the power of love.

Second John: A warning about false teachers.

Third John: Christian hospitality.

Jude: False "brethren" in the church; contending for the faith.

Revelation: Things to come; a book of praise to the One Who is worthy.

Chapter 16
Brief Dictionary

This dictionary is designed to give meanings to Christian words not found in normal secular English and not to be used with any specific translation of the Bible. It will be of some use with any translation that you may choose to use.

Abba: An Aramaic word for "father." Actually, a more precise definition would be "daddy." It has the meaning of knowing someone personally. It was with this word that Jesus addressed the Father: *"And he said, Abba, Father, all things are possible unto thee; take away this cup from me: nevertheless not what I will, but what thou wilt"* (Mark 14:36). Paul also uses this word in Romans 8:15 and Galatians 4:6.

Alien: Refers to a Christian who is in the world but not of the world. *"Beloved, I beg you, as foreigners and resident aliens, to shun the passions of the flesh which war against the soul"* (1 Peter 2:11 — Riverside).

Amen: A Hebrew word which, when it is used at the beginning of a statement or discourse, meant verily. For example when Jesus would say, "Verily, verily I say unto you," He was saying, "Amen, amen I say unto you." That sounds a little funny to most of us, for we put the amen at the end, which is like a signing off point. One literal meaning of amen is, "So be it."

Angel: Literally means "a messenger." More specifically, it refers to a heavenly being sent from God. It is commonly thought that all angels have wings, but this is not so. *"Be not forgetful to entertain strangers: for thereby some have entertained angels unawares"* (Heb. 13:2). One would not be unaware if the angel had wings. Also, when angels appeared to Old Testament saints, they nearly always appeared in the form of a man. A few times the word "angel" is used to describe one who is a messenger of Satan, as in Second Corinthians 12:7.

Antichrist: Specifically speaking, Antichrist is known as the "man of lawlessness" and "the lawless one." (2 Thess. 2:3,8,9.) He will deceive many by signs and lying wonders (2 Thess. 2:9,10). Jesus worked miracles through the power of God, and the Jews credited them to Satan (Matt. 12:24); the Antichrist will work miracles through satanic power, and will be worshipped by many as God. John gives a more general meaning in his writings. Compare First John 2:18, First John 4:3, and Second John 1:7.

Anointed: To anoint means to pour oil upon. Spiritually speaking, oil represents the Holy Spirit; therefore, when we speak of one being anointed, we mean that the Holy Spirit is upon him.

Apostles: Literally "sent forth," this word is what the Jews called those who carried letters from their rulers. In the New Testament, "apostle" is used to denote those whom Jesus has sent forth to proclaim the Gospel in places where it was not previously accepted. Originally there were twelve, but the New Testament speaks of twenty-one apostles in all.

Apostles are still in the Church today, but there will never be any who replace the Apostles of the Lamb, that is, the original Twelve. They are still sent forth by the Lord Jesus Christ with the mission to proclaim the Gospel. Many see the missionary as a modern-day apostle, but this is usually only partially true. A missionary is a sent one as well and may display many of the signs of an apostle, but a missionary generally stays pretty much in one place for a long period of time.

Some believe that apostles have authority over any local church, and that they can come in and tell the pastor what to do and how to run the church. A pastor, however, always has the authority in his church, and answers only to the Lord Jesus Christ.

Aramaic: A language very similar to Hebrew. It was the language that was spoken by many of the Jews.

Baptism: For the believer, water baptism symbolizes his death, burial, and resurrection with Christ (Rom. 6:3,4; Col. 2:12). Baptism means to immerse into something, as in the case just cited, water. Some also call forms such as sprinkling or pouring, baptism. These methods were practiced by the Early Church when a source of water could not be found.

There are other types of baptisms which are important to the believer as well, the most significant one being his baptism into the Body of Christ, which is performed by the Holy Spirit (1 Cor. 12:13; Gal. 3:27). Also, there is the baptism of the Holy Spirit which is performed by Jesus Himself (Matt. 3:11; Mark 1:8; Luke 3:16).

Blasphemy: Generally, blasphemy means speaking against God. Jesus said that attributing the miracles of Christ to Satan was blaspheming against the Holy Spirit (Matt. 12:22-32; Mark 3:22-30).

Blessed: Speaks of one whose life is fulfilled in things both temporal and spiritual.

Brother: Used to show either a blood relationship or a spiritual relationship — for example, brothers in Christ.

Children: Naturally speaking, the offspring of human parents. Spiritually, used to show our relationship to our divine Father, God. John called the believers who sat under him "little children."

Christ: A Greek word meaning the "Anointed One." Means the same as the Hebrew word "Messiah."

Church: This never means a building or denomination according to the New Testament. We may use it this way in our common English, but actually the word "Church" refers to a people who are called out or separated from the world. Scripture speaks of two churches, the church universal and the local church. A believer needs to belong to both. We enter the church universal by being born again; we belong to a local church so that we can fellowship with other Christians. Believers need to attend a local church where the Lord places them.

Codex: The predecessor of the modern book, it was formed by folding various sheets of papyrus in the middle, then binding them together at the fold.

Concise: Brief and to the point.

Corban: This is a Jewish term which literally means "an offering." This offering or sacrifice could be anything, an animal, land, or any other possession. This word was often used in connection with vows. If someone said to another to whom he owed money, "My property is corban to you," this meant that his property was a consecrated gift to God, thus preventing that one to whom he owed money from reaping any benefit from the property. This was very much approved of as a vow by many of the Pharisees, which led to abuse. Examples may be found in Matthew 15:5 and Mark 7:11.

Cornerstone: The cornerstone was a very large stone used at one end of a building. It was this stone that gave stability to the whole building. Scripture speaks of Jesus being our cornerstone. *"And are built upon the foundation of the apostles and prophets, Jesus Christ himself being the chief corner stone"* (Eph. 2:20).

Covenant: A legal contract ratified by blood. In the Old Testament this was done by means of circumcision. Today true circumcision is done on the heart. *"For the true Jew is not the* *man who is simply a Jew outwardly, and true circumcision is not that which is outward and bodily. But the true Jew is one inwardly, and true circumcision is heart-circumcision — not literal, but spiritual; and such people receive praise not from men, but from God"* (Rom. 2:28,29 *Weymouth*). The shed blood of our Lord Jesus Christ is what ratifies our covenant with God today. *See* E. W. Kenyon's book, *The Blood Covenant.*

Demon: An unclean spirit, sometimes called an evil spirit. The devil, or Satan, is the name of the chief demon, and when the Bible refers to one who has a devil it is referring to one who is under the influence of a demon. A person may be possessed by a demon, tormented by a demon, oppressed by a demon, or made ill by a demon. A Christian, however, can never be possessed by a demon because he is already possessed by the Holy Spirit.

Decapolis: Literally means "ten cities." A group of ten cities, nine of them were east of the Jordan River, while the tenth lay to west.

Denaruis: This was a Roman coin made of silver, about a day's wage.

Drachma: A silver coin of Greek origin. This was the basic Greek coin and was worth a day's wage.

Ecumenical: The ecumenical body of believers believe in a worldwide church. They are concerned with establishing unity among churches and other religions, often seeking unity at almost any cost.

Elder: In the New Testament there are approximately thirty references to the elders of the Old Testament. The term "elder" is a carry-over from Old Testament times when the elders were the overseers of the synagogue. It literally means "older man." In the New Testament, elders were first appointed to oversee the congregation (church) until a pastor could be appointed for that particular group. Today, elders are those set in the church by Jesus who assist the pastor with both spiritual and natural duties. The larger the church, the more elders there will be.

Etymological: Etymological refers to the history of a word.

Evangelical: Evangelicals are followers of Christ who believe in the exclusive authority and divine inspiration of the Bible. They believe in salvation only through regeneration by the blood of Jesus Christ, and in a spiritual transformation as evidenced by the fruit of the spirit. They are characterized by a zeal for soul-winning.

Faith: The classic definition of faith is found in Hebrews 11:1. *The Amplified New Testament* states that faith is ". . . perceiving as real fact what is not revealed to the senses." Faith is a matter of the heart and not the head; therefore, faith will work when the Word of God is in your heart, and yet doubt is attacking your mind and senses.

Fasting: The Bible refers to fasting generally as the practice of denying one's self of food for spiritual purposes. At times this may even include the drinking of water (Esther 4:16,17). The Bible also mentions the laying aside of only certain foods, as seen in Daniel 10:2,3.

The Bible does not say how long we are to fast, only that when Jesus mentions it to His disciples He says, *"Moreover when ye fast, be not, as the hypocrites, of a sad countenance: for they disfigure their faces, that they may appear unto men to fast. Verily I say unto you, They have their reward"* (Matt. 6:16). He says this the same way that He says, and ". . . *when ye pray* . . ." (Matt. 6:7) Jesus expects us to fast in the same way He expects us to pray.

Feast: Refers to a religious ceremony, most usually the Passover. Other feasts are mentioned as well, although not as often. John 7:2 talks about the Feast of the Tabernacles and

John 10:22 mentions the Feast of Dedication. Another feast mentioned in the New Testament is the Feast of Pentecost, also known as the Feast of Harvest, or Day of Firstfruits or the Feast of Weeks.

Firstfruits: The Jews practiced consecrating the first produce of the harvest as well as the first-born males of both men and animals. Believers are spoken of as being the firstfruits by their new birth through faith in Christ.

Flesh: Sometimes means the body, or if in reference to food, the flesh would be meat. In the writings of Paul where flesh is contrasted against the spirit, flesh generally means *the soul and the body working together against the spirit.* Paul tells us that this is, *"Because the carnal mind* [the mind of the flesh — *AP] is enmity against God: for it is not subject to the law of God, neither indeed can be"* (Rom. 8:7).

Gentiles: Anyone outside the Jewish race was considered a Gentile by the Jews. Gentiles were commonly looked down upon by the devout Jews. The Holy Spirit gives us His opinion of Gentiles in Romans 4:18. Quoting from Beet's marginal rendering out of his commentary on Romans, "Who (Abraham) against hope believed in hope, in order that he might become father of many Gentiles, according to the spoken word, so shall be thy seed."

Glory: The primary meaning of this word is brightness, splendor, radiance, especially in reference to the Presence of God. It is sometimes synonymous with the Spirit of God. Observe the following references:

> **ROMANS 6:4**
> 4   Therefore we are buried with him by baptism into death: that like as CHRIST WAS RAISED UP FROM THE DEAD BY THE GLORY OF THE FATHER, even so we also should walk in newness of life.

ROMANS 8:11
**11 But if THE SPIRIT OF HIM THAT RAISED UP
JESUS FROM THE DEAD dwell in you, he that
raised up Christ from the dead shall also quicken
your mortal bodies by his Spirit that dwelleth in
you.**

Gospel: The word "Gospel" has been translated "Good
News," "Glad Tidings" and "Joyful Message" by various translators. It refers to the Kingdom of God and includes salvation,
peace, safety, preservation, prosperity, health, and eternal life
through the death, burial, and resurrection of Jesus.

Grace: God's undeserved and free love, mercy and kind-
ness, and all that benefits mankind through Jesus Christ.
Under grace we have an open relationship with the Father
through Christ.

Hallowed: To be set apart or made holy for the Lord.

Herodians: A political party in Israel, so named for their
allegiance to the Herod dynasty, which lasted approximately
one hundred years and was at its height during the time of
Christ.

Holy: There are two aspects to holiness. The first is to be
separated from all that is not of the Lord, and the second one
is to be true to all that the Lord is. The Greek word that is
translated "holy," which is the root word for "sanctification," is
the same word which is rendered "saint" in other passages of
Scripture.

Holy Ghost/Spirit: The Holy Ghost and Holy Spirit are
one and the same. He is the Third Person of the Godhead,
sometimes referred to simply as the Spirit. The main work of
the Holy Spirit today includes wooing the lost unto Christ and
teaching and bringing comfort to the believer.

Homiletic: Homiletic means the art of preaching.

Hosanna: Means "save now," or "save, we pray."

MATTHEW 21:9
9 And the multitudes that went before, and that followed, cried, saying, Hosanna to the Son of David: Blessed is he that cometh in the name of the Lord; Hosanna in the highest.

This was the usual form of praise at the Feast of Tabernacles.

PSALM 118:25,26
25 Save now, I beseech thee, O Lord: O Lord, I beseech thee, send now prosperity.
26 Blessed be he that cometh in the name of the Lord: we have blessed you out of the house of the Lord.

Idol: Generally speaking, an idol is anything in our lives that we esteem more highly than Christ. Too often, things can become idols to us without our even realizing it. We can make idols of anything, including working for God (instead of working with God), spouses, children, career, recreational time, money, church, food and social standing.

Infirmity: A weakness or inability. Seldom refers to sickness.

Intercession: Going to God in prayer for the benefit of someone else.

Jot: The smallest letter of the Hebrew alphabet.

Kingdom of God/Kingdom of Heaven: The phrase "kingdom of heaven" is found 32 times in 31 verses and every single occurrence is found in the Gospel of Matthew. In the other two synoptic gospels, Mark and Luke, we see the phrase "kingdom of God" used in the same parable or setting. Matthew's Gospel is a Gospel to the Jewish people, and since the Jews did not like to use the name of God in their conversation, believing that it was too holy for common speech, the Holy Spirit had Matthew use the term "kingdom of heaven" in his Gospel.

Lasciviousness: Indecent conduct (Gal. 5:19).

Law: The Law is the revealed will of God for the Jew, and is recorded in the first five books of the Old Testament. Sometimes called the Five Books of Moses.

Law and the Prophets: The sacred writings of the Jews. They were actually two of the three sections that make up the Old Testament, the third being the Psalms.

Lord of Hosts: This title of God originally meant that He was the Lord of the armies of Israel. After several years it came to signify the omnipotence of God the Father.

Leper: A leper is one who suffers from a contagious skin disease. He was considered unclean according to the Jewish Law.

Levite: A Levite was a member of the priestly tribe of Levi.

Lust: A strong desire for something contrary to God's will.

Mammon: This is an Aramaic word which, according to many scholars, means "the god of riches."

Messiah: The title of Messiah is a Hebrew term for the One coming to set up God's Kingdom. It literally means, "The Anointed One." The title "Christ" is the Greek equivalent.

Nuance: A nuance refers to the various shades of meaning that a word may have.

Parable: A parable is an allegory in story form which is used to illustrate an important truth or spiritual concept.

Paraclete: Used as a title of the Holy Spirit in every reference except one, where it is a reference to Jesus (John 14:16). It is translated "comforter" four times and "advocate" once in the *King Jaines Version* of the New Testament. This word means one who is summoned, or called to one's side. The

Holy Spirit has taken the place of Christ in the earth, leading and guiding believers into a deeper relationship with Jesus, and strengthening the believer to undergo trials, tribulations, and persecutions. When speaking of Jesus in John 14:16, it refers to His glorification at God's right hand, pleading with God the Father for the pardon of our sins.

Passover: The Passover feast lasted from the fourteenth to the twenty-first day of the month of Nisan. It was during this time that the Passover lamb was slain and eaten according to the instructions given in Exodus 12, Numbers 9, and Deuteronomy 16. This is also known as the Feast of Unleavened Bread. John the Baptist refers to Jesus as the Passover Lamb in John 1:29: *"The next day John seeth Jesus coming unto him, and saith, Behold the LAMB OF GOD, which taketh away the sin of the world."*

Paul uses this term in First Corinthians 5:7: *"Purge out therefore the old leaven, that ye may be a new lump, as ye are unleavened. For even CHRIST our PASSOVER is sacrificed for us."*

Pharisees: A body of pious followers of the Law. They were organized during the Macabean period for the purpose of preserving the Word of God. During the course of time they lost the vision that God had given to them and instituted their own rules and interpretation of the Law. Many of the Pharisees were saved and became Christians. One of the most famous Pharisees was the Apostle Paul.

Praetorium: This was the palace where the Roman governor or procurator of a province lived.

Priest: The priests were responsible for the daily services and sacrifices in the Temple.

Prophesy: To speak in an inspired utterance given by the Holy Spirit. In the New Testament, prophesying has nothing to do with speaking of the future, rather it is given *for edification,* *and exhortation, and comfort* (1 Cor. 14:3). (*Prophecy* is the noun form — that which is prophesied.)

Rabbi: Rabbi is a Hebrew word which means "master," or "teacher."

Raca: This was a senseless, empty-headed man. An insult used among the Jews in the time of Christ.

Repentance: Repentance is a changing of the mind, a turning around and going in the other direction.

Right, righteous, righteousness: The believer has been made right with God through his relationship with God in Christ. Righteousness means that we have no sense of guilt, sin, or condemnation because of what Jesus has done. We need to be conscious of sin, but not sin conscious. The words justice, just, and justify are from the exact same Greek word.

Publican: The publicans were Jewish tax collectors engaged by the Roman authorities.

Sabbath: Sabbath is the Hebrew and Aramaic name of the seventh day of the week which God had set aside as a day of rest for man. A Sabbath year, then, is the seventh year, which was set aside for the ground to rest from the crops.

Sadducees: The Sadducees were an aristocratic circle of men who were slack in their doctrines and beliefs. They did not believe in angels or in the resurrection of the dead (Acts 23:6-8).

Sanhedrin: The Sanhedrin was a local Jewish court made up mainly of priests and scribes.

Scroll: A roll of parchment or papyrus used for writing a document in ancient times.

Scribe: Scribes were a group of people who knew the Mosaic Law and the Sacred Writings. They would explain, administer, and teach the Law. They were also called doctors of the law (Luke 5:17) and lawyers (Luke 10:25).

Sign: A sign is a miracle which discloses a significant meaning to the ones who see it. For instance, one may see healing as a sign and accept Jesus as their Lord. Signs are not used to lead or guide the believer. Believers are to be lead by the Word of God and the Holy Spirit.

Son of Man: Son of Man is a title used by Jesus when speaking of Himself, meaning that He is the representative Man, the last Adam.

Synagogue: This was a building where Jews would assemble together to pray, as well as to listen to the reading and explanation of the Scriptures. Synagogues were established after the Babylonian exile wherever there were any Jews. The synagogue was also used for holding trials, and sometimes even for administering punishments.

Talent: A sum of money that weighs a talent, usually silver or gold.

Teacher: *See* Rabbi.

Temple-tax: A tax assessment placed on all Jews for the maintenance and upkeep of the Temple. The amount was two drachmas.

Unclean spirit: *See* demon.

Winnowing fan: A winnowing fan was a shovel like tool used to toss wheat stalks, which, having been crushed on a round stone floor, would be thrown into the air. The wind would then blow away the chaff, which was lighter, and the wheat would fall to the ground. From there the wheat could be gathered and taken to storage.

Wrath: Wrath simply shows God's attitude toward sin. Sinners are the ones who bring God's wrath upon themselves, for God sent Jesus to die for them and bring them into a relationship with Himself.

Part V

Scriptures on God's Word

Chapter 17

Benefits of Spending Time In God's Word

A Study in Psalm 119

All scripture references in this chapter are taken from the New American Standard Bible.

God's blessing is upon those who observe His testimonies and keep His statutes:

> **PSALM 119:1-5**
> How blessed are those whose way is blameless, who walk in the law of the Lord. How blessed are those who observe His testimonies, who seek Him with all their heart. They also do no unrighteousness; they walk in His ways. Thou hast ordained Thy precepts, that we should keep them diligently. Oh that my ways may be established to keep Thy statutes!

Treasuring God's Word in My Heart Keeps Me From Sin:

> **PSALM 119:9-11**
> How can a young man keep his way pure? By keeping it according to Thy word. With all my heart I have sought Thee; do not let me wander from Thy commandments. Thy word I have treasured in my heart, that I may not sin against Thee.

God's Word Gives Me Council:

PSALM 119:24
Thy testimonies also are my delight; they are my
counselors.

Spending Time in God's Word Produces Reverence for
God:

PSALM 119:38
Establish Thy word to Thy servant, as that which
produces reverence for Thee.

God's Word Keeps Me From Shame:

PSALM 119:46
I will also speak of Thy testimonies before kings,
and shall not be ashamed:

God's Word Comforts and Revives Me:

PSALM 119:50
This is my comfort in my affliction, that Thy word
has revived me.

God's Word Causes Me to Give Thanks:

PSALM 119:61,62
The cords of the wicked have encircled me, but I
have not forgotten Thy law. At midnight I shall rise
to give thanks to Thee because of Thy righteous
ordinances.

God's Word Teaches Me Discernment and Knowledge:

PSALM 119:66
Teach me good discernment and knowledge, for I
believe in Thy commandments.

God's Word Preserves Me From Destruction:

PSALM 119:87
They almost destroyed me on earth, but as for me,
I did not forsake Thy precepts.

God's Word Keeps Me Spiritually Recharged:

PSALM 119:93
I will never forget Thy precepts, for by them Thou
hast revived me.

God's Word Gives Me Wisdom and Understanding:

PSALM 119:98-100
Thy commandments make me wiser than my ene-
mies, for they are ever mine. I have more insight
than all my teachers, for Thy testimonies are my
meditation. I understand more than the aged,
because I have observed Thy precepts.

The Testimonies of the Lord Are the Joy of My Heart:

PSALM 119:111
I have inherited Thy testimonies forever, for they
are the joy of my heart.

God's Word Sustains Me and Gives Me Life:

PSALM 119:116
Sustain me according to Thy word, that I may live;
and do not let me be ashamed of my hope.

Sin Will Not Have Dominion Over Me:

PSALM 119:133
Establish my footsteps in Thy word, and do not let
any iniquity have dominion over me.

God's Word is My Delight In the Face of Trouble:

> **PSALM 119:143**
> **Trouble and anguish have come upon me; yet Thy
> commandments are my delight.**

God's Word Pleads My Cause and Rescues Me:

> **PSALM 119:153,154**
> **Look upon my affliction and rescue me, for I do not
> forget Thy law. Plead my cause and redeem me;
> revive me according to Thy word.**

God's Word Fills Me With Peace and Keeps Me From
Stumbling:

> **PSALM 119:165**
> **Those who love Thy law have great peace, and
> nothing causes them to stumble.**

God's Word Brings Me Back When I Stray:

> **PSALM 119:176**
> **I have gone astray like a lost sheep; seek Thy ser-
> vant, for I do not forget Thy commandments.**

Chapter 18
The Word of God As a Seed

A Study of the Parable of the Sower — Mark 4

All Scripture references are taken from KJV unless otherwise noted.

The Word of God is Seed Sown in Our Hearts:

> **MARK 4:14**
> 14 The sower soweth the word.

> **MARK 4:14** (*Crofts*)
> The seed represents God's message to men, and the sower those who preach it.

> **MARK 4:14** (*Noli*)
> Well, the sower sows the Gospel.

The Devil Comes to Steal What is Sown in Our Hearts:

> **MARK 4:15**
> 15 And these are they by the way side, where the word is sown; but when they have heard, Satan cometh immediately, and taketh away the word that was sown in their hearts.

> **MARK 4:15** (*Crofts*)
> The hard ground of the path pictures those who hear the message, but don't understand it. Then lest they should finally grasp it and believe and be saved, Satan comes and withdraws their attention from what they've heard.

MARK 4:15 (*Johnson*)
Planting on the hard earth is like an encounter
with a person whose response to the witness is
superficial; thus, there is no penetration of his
defenses. Immediately the Adversary snatches
away the impact of the encounter.

The Word Can Leave by Being Offended:

MARK 4:16,17
16 And these are they likewise which are sown on
stony ground; who, when they have heard the
word, immediately receive it with gladness;
17 And have no root in themselves, and so endure
but for a time: afterward, when affliction or persecution ariseth for the word's sake, immediately
they are offended.

MARK 4:16,17 (*Goddard*)
Some hear the Good News with joy, but it does not
sink very deep into their stony hearts. It endures
for a time, but when persecution and testing come
because of it, they quickly falter. This is the seed
that falls on rocky places.

MARK 4:16,17 (*Johnson*)
Those persons who are represented by the thin
layer of earth are those who immediately celebrate an encounter with an authentic communica-
tor of God. But the joy is short-lived because they
do not open their inner being to the presentation
of the Spirit, and soon the surface encounter with-
ers.

MARK 4:16,17 (*Crofts*)
The rock thinly covered with soil stands for those
who hear the message and accept it enthusiasti-
cally. But these people have no stability. They do
well for a time, but if they meet troubles or difficulties or have to face persecution for their faith,
they grow discouraged and fall away.

The Word Can Leave When Other Things Come Before God:

MARK 4:18,19
18 And these are they which are sown among thorns; such as hear the word,
19 And the cares of this world, and the deceitfulness of riches, and the lusts of other things entering in, choke the word, and it becometh unfruitful.

MARK 4:18,19 (*Johnson*)
Those seed sown among thorns are like encounters with persons who are possessed with wealth or pleasure, whose awareness is on externals, and these other interests quickly erase the impact of the encounter.

MARK 4:18,19 (Goddard)
18 Then there are those that hear the Good News and welcome it after a fashion; but the natural cares of life, the deceitfulness of riches, the desire for other things, all come in to crowd it out. This is the seed that falls among thorns.

MARK 4:18,19 (*Crofts*)
18 The weedy patch portrays those who also hear and accept the message. These persons' minds are full of worldly cares. They are occupied with their money and their pleasures, so that their spiritual aspirations are stifled and their lives grow no better.

The Result of Receiving the Word of God:

MARK 4:20
20 And these are they which are sown on good ground; such as hear the word, and receive it, and bring forth fruit, some thirtyfold, some sixty, and some an hundred.

MARK 4:20 (*Johnson*)
The seed sown on good ground are those encounters in which there is a real meeting of

persons, those in which each feels himself or herself to be met by God. These seed then are received, they grow and bear fruit — some thirty, some sixty, and some a hundred times as much as the initial planting.

MARK 4:20 (*Goddard*)
But the seed falls in good ground when they that hear the Good News appreciate it and accept it in good and humble hearts, and who hold it firmly and patiently until it brings forth fruit in their lives.

MARK 4:20 (*Crofts*)
The good land represents those who hear and understand and accept the message. With honesty of purpose they hold it fast and act upon it with perseverance. It is these who bear the fruit, some thirty, some sixty, and some a hundredfold.

Chapter 19

What Jesus and Others Said About the Word

What Jesus Said About the Word

DEUTERONOMY 8:3
3 And he humbled thee, and suffered thee to hunger, and fed thee with manna, which thou knewest not, neither did thy fathers know, that he might make thee know that man doth not live by bread only, but by every word that proceedeth out of the mouth of the Lord doth man live.

Jesus quotes Deuteronomy 8:3 from the Old Testament. We find it in Matthew 4:4 and Luke 4:4. We will use them both.

MATTHEW 4:4
4 But he answered and said, It is written, Man shall not live by bread alone, but by every word that proceedeth out of the mouth of God.

MATTHEW 4:4 (*Hurault*)
But Jesus answered, "Scripture says: people cannot live on bread alone, they need every word that God speaks."

MATTHEW 4:4 (*Barclay*)
Jesus answered, "Scripture says: 'It takes more than bread to keep a man alive; man's life depends on every word that God speaks."

LUKE 4:4
And Jesus answered him, saying, It is written, That man shall not live by bread alone, but by every word of God.

LUKE 4:4 (*Templeton*)
"No," Jesus said. "The scriptures teach that life is more than food; a man must also feed his spirit on God's words."

JOHN 15:7
7 If ye abide in me, and my words abide in you, ye shall ask what ye will, and it shall be done unto you.

JOHN 15:7 (*Williams*)
If you remain in union with me and my words remain in you, you may ask whatever you please and you shall have it.

JOHN 15:7 (*Matheny*)
If you take up your dwelling in Me (start living in fellowship with Me), and My words start abiding in you, whatever you are wishing — ask at once for yourselves, and it shall be done for you.

JOHN 6:63
63 It is the spirit that quickeneth; the flesh profiteth nothing: the words that I speak unto you, they are spirit, and they are life.

JOHN 6:63 (*Wade*)
It is the Spirit that creates true Life; mere flesh is of no avail. The words that I have spoken to you are Spiritual in their meaning, and Life-giving in their effects.

JOHN 6:63 (*Riggs*)
Is it not always the spirit, and the spirit alone, that is life-giving? "Flesh," without it has no abiding value; it is like manna. All the words through which I have offered myself to you are meant to be channels of the spirit and of life to you, since in believing those words you would be brought into contact with the life in me.

What an Angel Said About the Word

LUKE 1:37
37 For with God nothing shall be impossible.

LUKE 1:37 (*Riverside*)
For no word that comes from God will fail.

LUKE 1:37 (*Montgomery*)
For no word of God shall be void of power.

What Paul Said About the Word

ROMANS 10:17
17 So then faith cometh by hearing, and hearing by the word of God.

ROMANS 10:17 (*NEB*)
We conclude that faith is awakened by the message, and the message that awakens it comes through the word of Christ.

ROMANS 10:17 (*Kasemann*)
So faith comes from the message heard, and the message (comes) in the power of the word of God.

COLOSSIANS 3:16
16 Let the word of Christ dwell in you richly in all wisdom; teaching and admonishing one another in psalms and hymns and spiritual songs, singing with grace in your hearts to the Lord.

COLOSSIANS 3:16 (*Hayman*)
Let the word of Christ dwell within you fruitfully. In all wisdom carry on mutual teaching, mutual instruction; by psalms, hymns, and devotional strains, singing in your hearts to God, as His grace enables you.

COLOSSIANS 3:16 (*Arthur Way*)
May the word Messiah speaks to you have in your hearts, in all its wealth, its home. With all

discretion teach and admonish one another. With psalms, with hymns, with chants inspired by the Spirit, be your hearts singing ever in thankfulness to God.

2 TIMOTHY 2:9
9   Wherein I suffer trouble, as an evil doer, even unto bonds; but the word of God is not bound.

2 TIMOTHY 2:9 (*Barclay*)
It is for the sake of that gospel that I am at present suffering, even to the length of being imprisoned as a criminal. But no one can put the word of God in prison.

2 TIMOTHY 2:9 (*MacKnight*)
For which gospel I suffer evil even to bonds as a malefactor. But though my enemies may bind me, they cannot bind the word of God. It will spread itself in spite of all opposition.

2 TIMOTHY 2:15
5   Study to shew thyself approved unto God, a workman that needeth not to be ashamed, rightly dividing the word of truth.

2 TIMOTHY 2:15 (*Moule*)
Be in earnest to present to God yourself, tested and true, a workman unashamed, holding straight onward through the Word of the truth.

2 TIMOTHY 2:15 (*Kent*)
Be diligent to present yourselves approved to God, a workman not needing to be ashamed, cutting straight the word of truth.

HEBREWS 4:12
12 For the word of God is quick, and powerful, and sharper than any twoedged sword, piercing even to the dividing asunder of soul and spirit, and of the joints and marrow, and is a discerner of the thoughts and intents of the heart.

HEBREWS 4:12 (*Swann*)
For the word of God is alive and active, and sharper than any two-edged sword; piercing to the division of soul and spirit; of joints and marrow, and able to judge the thoughts and intentions of heart.

HEBREWS 4:12 (*Thomas Sheldon Green*)
For living is the word of God and full of power, and sharper than every two-edged sword, and piercing to a cleaving asunder of soul and spirit and of joints and marrow, and quick to scan ponderings and thoughts of the heart.

HEBREWS 4:12 (Moffatt)
For the Logos of God is a living thing, active and more cutting than any sword with double edge, penetrating to the very division of soul and spirit, joints and marrow — scrutinizing the very thoughts and conceptions of the heart.

What James Said About the Word

JAMES 1:21-24
21 Wherefore lay apart all filthiness and super-fluity of naughtiness, and receive with meekness the engrafted word, which is able to save your souls.
22 But be ye doers of the word, and not hearers only, deceiving your own selves.
23 For if any be a hearer of the word, and not a doer, he is like unto a man beholding his natural face in a glass:
24 For he beholdeth himself, and goeth his way, and straightway forgetteth what manner of man he was.

JAMES 1:21-24 (*Rotherham 2nd Edition*)
Wherefore, putting away all filth and remainder of wickedness, in meekness welcome ye the word adapted for inward growth, which has power to save your souls. But become ye word-doers, and not hearers only, reasoning yourselves astray.

Because, if any one is a word-hearer, and not a
doer, the same resembles a man observing his natural face in a mirror; for he observed himself, and
away has gone! and, straightway, it escaped him of
what sort he was.

JAMES 1:21-24 (*Moffatt*)
So clear away all the foul rank growth of malice,
and make a soil of modesty for the Word which
roots itself inwardly with power to save your
souls. Act on the Word, instead of merely listening
to it and deluding yourselves. For whoever listens
and does nothing, is like a man who glances at his
natural face in a mirror; he glances at himself,
goes off, and at once forgets what he was like.

What Peter Said About the Word

1 PETER 1:23
23 Being born again, not of corruptible seed, but
of incorruptible, by the word of God, which liveth
and abideth for ever.

1 PETER 1:23 (*Laubach*)
You have been born again. This new birth did not
come from the seed of a man's body, which soon
dies. Your second birth came from the living word
of God which never dies.

1 PETER 1:23 (*Julian Anderson*)
Because you have been born again by the living
and eternal Word of God. And therefore you are
not children of a human father, who must die, but
of a Father who can never die.

1 PETER 1:25
25 But the word of the Lord endureth for ever.
And this is the word which by the gospel is
preached unto you.

1 PETER 1:25 (*Knox*)
But the word of the Lord lasts for ever. And this
word is nothing other than the gospel which has
been preached to you.

1 PETER 1:25 (*Adams*)
"But the Lord's Word remains forever." Now, this is the Word that was announced to you as good news.

What John Said About the Word

1 JOHN 2:14
14 I have written unto you, fathers, because ye have known him that is from the beginning. I have written unto you, young men, because ye are strong, and the word of God abideth in you, and ye have overcome the wicked one.

1 JOHN 2:14 (*Norlie*)
Let me repeat it: I have written to you, fathers, because you know Him who has always existed from the beginning. I have written to you, young men, because you are strong and God's Word is treasured in your hearts, and because you have overcome the evil one.

1 JOHN 2:14 (*Laubach*)
Fathers, I write to you because you know the Christ who lived before the world began. Young men, I write to you because you are strong. The word of God lives in you, and you have defeated the Evil One.

REVELATION 19:13
13 And he was clothed with a vesture dipped in blood: and his name is called The Word of God.

REVELATION 19:13 (*Wuest*)
And his name has been called, and the name is on record, The Word of God.

REVELATION 19:13 (*Fenton*)
And was dressed in a robe sprinkled with blood; and His appointed title is — THE WORD OF GOD.

Chapter 20

The Word of God Speaks of Itself

The Bible Was Written By God

ROMANS 15:4
4 For whatsoever things were written aforetime were written for our learning, that we through patience and comfort of the scriptures might have hope.

ROMANS 15:4 (*Weymouth*)
For all that was written of old has been written for our instruction, so that we may always have hope through the power of endurance and the encouragement which the Scriptures afford.

ROMANS 15:4 (*Simple English*)
Everything that was written long ago was written to teach us. We should learn that we can have hope through the patience and comfort from the Scriptures.

1 CORINTHIANS 2:13
13 Which things also we speak, not in the words which man's wisdom teacheth, but which the Holy Ghost teacheth; comparing spiritual things with spiritual.

1 CORINTHIANS 3:13 (*TLB*)
In telling you about these gifts we have even used the very words given to us by the Holy Spirit, not words that we as men might choose. So we use the

Holy Spirit's words to explain the Holy Spirit's facts.

1 CORINTHIANS 3:13 (*Weymouth*)
Of these we speak — not in language which man's wisdom teaches us, but in that which the Spirit teaches — adapting, as we do, spiritual words to spiritual truths.

1 CORINTHIANS 10:11
11 Now all these things happened unto them for ensamples: and they are written for our admonition, upon whom the ends of the world are come.

1 CORINTHIANS 10:11 (*Montgomery*)
Now these things were happening to them typically, but were written down for our admonition who stand at the meeting of the ages.

1 CORINTHIANS 10:11 (*Rotherham*)
But these things by way of type were happening unto them, and were written with a view to our admonition, unto whom the ends of the ages have reached along.

1 CORINTHIANS 10:11 (*Conybeare*)
Now these things befell them as shadows of things to come; and they were written for our warning, on whom the ends of the ages are come.

EPHESIANS 6:17
17 And take the helmet of salvation, and the sword of the Spirit, which is the word of God.

EPHESIANS 6:17 (*Goodspeed*)
And take salvation for your helmet, and for your sword the Spirit, which is the voice of God.

EPHESIANS 6:17 (*Rotherham*)
And the helmet of salvation welcome ye, and the sword of the spirit, which is what God hath spoken.

2 TIMOTHY 3:16,17
16 All scripture is given by inspiration of God, and is profitable for doctrine, for reproof, for correction, for instruction in righteousness:
17 That the man of God may be perfect, throughly furnished unto all good works.

2 TIMOTHY 3:16,17 (*Weymouth*)
Every Scripture is inspired by God and is useful for teaching, for convincing, for correction of error, and for instruction in right doing; so that the man of God may himself be complete and may be perfectly equipped for every good work.

2 TIMOTHY 3:16,17 (*NIV*)
All Scripture is God-breathed and is useful for teaching, rebuking, correcting and training in righteousness, so that the man of God may be thoroughly equipped for every good work.

2 PETER 1:20,21
20 Knowing this first, that no prophecy of the scripture is of any private interpretation.
21 For the prophecy came not in old time by the will of man: but holy men of God spake as they were moved by the Holy Ghost.

2 PETER 1:20,21 (*Weymouth*)
But, above all, remember that no prophecy in Scripture will be found to have come from the prophet's own prompting; for never did any prophecy come by human will, but men sent by God spoke as they were impelled by the Holy Spirit.

2 PETER 1:20,21 (*Simple English*)
This is the most important thing you should know: No prophecy of Scripture ever came about by a prophet's own ideas, because prophecy never came from what man wanted. No, those men spoke from God while they were being influenced by the Holy Spirit.

The Value and Power of the Word

DEUTERONOMY 32:2
2   My doctrine shall drop as the rain, my speech shall distill as the dew, as the small rain upon the tender herb, and as the showers upon the grass.

DEUTERONOMY 32:2 (*TLB*)
My words shall fall upon you like the gentle rain and dew, like rain upon the tender grass, like showers on the hillside.

DEUTERONOMY 32:2 (*Knox*)
There is teaching big with import as the rain, here are warnings that must soak in like the dew, wholesome as sowers are to the grass, as moisture to the growing crops.

PSALM 12:6
6   The words of the Lord are pure words: as silver tried in a furnace of earth, purified seven times.

PSALM 12:6 (*Grimes*)
The Lord speaks and his holy words are pure, they ring like silver seven times refined.

PSALM 12:6 (*Callan*)
The promises of the Lord are sincere; they are like silver refined in a furnace, flowing out to earth, completely purified.

PSALM 19:7-10
7   The law of the Lord is perfect, converting the soul: the testimony of the Lord is sure, making wise the simple.
8   The statutes of the Lord are right, rejoicing the heart: the commandment of the Lord is pure, enlightening the eyes.
9   The fear of the Lord is clean, enduring for ever: the judgments of the Lord are true and righteous altogether.

10 More to be desired are they than gold, yea, than much fine gold: sweeter also than honey and the honeycomb.

PSALM 19:7-10 (*Noli*)
Perfect is the Torah of the Lord, for his doctrines make the simple wise and restore our minds and souls; for his precepts give our hearts great joy; his commandments give us light; for his faith is pure and everlasting; for his rules are true and right-eous, more beloved than gold, than much fine gold; sweeter than sweet honey and honeycomb.

PSALM 19:7-10 (*Zerr*)
The instruction of Yahweh is complete, restoring my soul. The command of Yahweh is reliable, giving wisdom to my mind. The precepts of Yahweh are right, gladdening my heart. The command of Yahweh is radiant, enlightening my eyes. The authority of Yahweh is clear; it stands firm forever. The judgments of Yahweh are true; every one of them is just. They are more desirable than gold — even the finest gold. They are sweeter than honey — even the sweetest honey.

PSALM 119:14
14 I have rejoiced in the way of thy testimonies, as much as in all riches.

PSALM 119:14 (*Cheyne*)
In the way of thy testimonies I have as great joy as in all manner of riches.

PSALM 119:14 (*Fenton*)
In pursuing Your proofs, I delighted as if over wealth.

PSALM 119:72
72 The law of thy mouth is better unto me than thousands of gold and silver.

PSALM 119:72 (*Revised Psalter*)
The law of thy mouth is dearer to me; than thousands of gold and silver pieces.

PSALM 119:103
103 How sweet are thy words unto my taste! yea,
sweeter than honey to my mouth!

PSALM 119:103 (*Zerr*)
How sweet your words are to my taste! They taste
better than honey to me.

PSALM 119:103 (*Noli*)
Oracles and sermons of the Lord are as sweet as
honey to the mouth.

PSALM 119:105
105 Thy word is a lamp unto my feet, and a light
unto my path.

PSALM 119:105 (*Grimes*)
I have no lamp to guide me save thy word, my path
was dark except for light from heaven.

PROVERBS 6:23
23 For the commandment is a lamp; and the law is
light; and reproofs of instruction are the way of
life.

PROVERBS 6:23 (*NIV*)
For these commands are a lamp, this teaching is a
light, and the corrections of discipline are the way
to life.

PROVERBS 6:23 (*NEB*)
For a command is a lamp, and teaching a light,
reproof and correction point the way of life.

PROVERBS 6:23 (*McFadyen*)
For precept illumines, instruction enlightens, and
reproof that disciplines leads unto life.

LUKE 8:11
11 Now the parable is this: The seed is the word of
God.

LUKE 8:11 (*Templeton*)
The seed itself is God's Word.

HEBREWS 4:12
12 For the word of God is quick, and powerful, and
sharper than any twoedged sword, piercing even
to the dividing asunder of soul and spirit, and of
the joints and marrow, and is a discerner of the
thoughts and intents of the heart.

HEBREWS 4:12 (*Shuttleworth*)
For the blessed covenant of the Gospel is endued
with an active and searching influence; it is not a
thing which can be lightly deemed of, but is sharper
than a two-edged sword, penetrating into the very
centre of the soul, and of its most secret thoughts;
exploring the whole interior of man's nature, and
detecting every feeling and apprehension of the
heart.

2 PETER 1:19
19 We have also a more sure word of prophecy;
whereunto ye do well that ye take heed, as unto a
light that shineth in a dark place, until the day
dawn, and the day star arise in your hearts.

2 PETER 1:19 (*P. G. PARKER*)
We have also an even more sure word from the
prophets of the Old Testament, to whom we do well
to take heed, even as we heed to a light which
shines in a dark place, until the dawn dispels all
the darkness, and Christ, like the morning-star,
dispels all doubt that the Eternal Day has dawned.

The Admonition of the Word

PSALM 119:9
9 Wherewithal shall a young man cleanse his
way? by taking heed thereto according to thy
word.

PSALM 119:9 (*RSV*)
How can a young man keep his way pure? By
guarding it according to thy word.

PSALM 119:9 (*Revised Psalter*)
How shall a young man keep himself undefiled;
even by ruling himself after thy word.

PSALM 119:11
11 Thy word have I hid in mine heart, that I might
not sin against thee.

PSALM 119:11 (*Noli*)
In my heart your Holy Word I treasure to protect
me from all sins against you.

PSALM 119:50
50 This is my comfort in my affliction: for thy
word hath quickened me.

PSALM 119:50 (*McFadyen*)
This is my comfort in trouble, that Thy word
giveth life unto me.

PSALM 119:130
130 The entrance of thy words giveth light; it
giveth understanding unto the simple.

PSALM 119:130 (*Noli*)
Lord, your Scriptures are enlightening, they make
simple people understand.

JOHN 15:3
3 Now ye are clean through the word which I
have spoken unto you.

JOHN 15:3 (*P. G. Parker*)
Now you have been pruned and cleansed by the
word I have spoken to you.

JOHN 15:3 (*Riggs*)
On account of the revelation of spiritual truth
which you have accepted, you are clean, that is, in

a fit condition to bear fruit; see to it that you keep in vital union with me.

JOHN 20:31
31 But these are written, that ye might believe that Jesus is the Christ, the Son of God; and that believing ye might have life through his name.

JOHN 20:31 (*AMP*)
But these are written (recorded) in order that you may believe that Jesus is the Christ, the Anointed One, the Son of God, and that through believing and cleaving to and trusting in and relying upon Him you may have life through (in) His name [that is, through what He is].

JOHN 20:31 (*Templeton*)
What is written here has been inscribed for one purpose: that you may believe that Jesus is the Christ, God's son, and believing this may, on his authority, have Life.

ACTS 20:32
32 And now, brethren, I commend you to God, and to the word of his grace, which is able to build you up, and to give you an inheritance among all them which are sanctified.

ACTS 20:32 (*G. W. Wade*)
And now I commend you to the Lord and to His gracious Message — to Him Who is able to elevate and fortify your characters, and to give you the promised Inheritance among all those who are sanctified.

1 THESSALONIANS 2:13
13 For this cause also thank we God without ceasing, because, when ye received the word of God which ye heard of us, ye received it not as the word of men, but as it is in truth, the word of God, which effectually worketh also in you that believe.

1 THESSALONIANS 2:13 (*Rutherford*)
There is still another reason why we give God
thanks perpetually. When You took from our lips
the word of God, you accepted it not as a word
from man, but as that which in fact it is, a word
from God, actually operative in you who believe.

EPHESIANS 5:26
26 That he might sanctify and cleanse it with the
washing of water by the word.

EPHESIANS 5:26 (*Knox*)
He would hallow it, purify it by bathing it in the
water to which his word gave life.

2 TIMOTHY 3:15-17
15 And that from a child thou hast known the holy
scriptures, which are able to make thee wise unto
salvation through faith which is in Christ Jesus.
16 All scripture is given by inspiration of God, and
is profitable for doctrine, for reproof, for correction, for instruction in righteousness:
17 That the man of God may be perfect, throughly
furnished unto all good works.

2 TIMOTHY 3:15-17 (*NIV*)
And how from infancy you have known the holy
Scriptures, which are able to make you wise for salvation through faith in Christ Jesus. All Scripture
is God-breathed and is useful for teaching, rebuking, correcting and training in righteousness, so
that the man of God may be thoroughly equipped
for every good work.

JAMES 1:21
21 Wherefore lay apart all filthiness and super-
fluity of naughtiness, and receive with meekness
the engrafted word, which is able to save your
souls.

JAMES 1:21 (*Swann*)
Then, having put away all filth and residue of
wickedness, in meekness accept the implanted
word which is able to save your souls.

JAMES 1:21 (*Baxter*)
Also cast away all filthiness out of your thoughts,
affections, speech, and practice, and all excremen-
titious naughtiness, (or that superfluity, which is
but provision for the flesh, to satisfy its lust;) and
with humble, tractable meekness, receive God's
word, not only opinionatively, but as the graft is
taken into the tree, or your food, when it is
digested into blood and flesh, thus made an innat-
uralized word; and so received and digested, it will
save your souls.

How To Put the Word of God To Use

DEUTERONOMY 6:6-9
6   And these words, which I command thee this
day, shall be in thine heart:
7   And thou shalt teach them diligently unto thy
children, and shalt talk of them when thou sittest in
thine house, and when thou walkest by the way, and
when thou liest down, and when thou risest up.
8   And thou shalt bind them for a sign upon thine
hand, and they shall be as frontlets between thine
eyes.
9   And thou shalt write them upon the posts of
thy house, and on thy gates.

DEUTERONOMY 6:6-9 (*Moffatt*)
These words you must learn by heart, this charge
of mine; you must impress them on your children,
you must talk about them when you are sitting at
home and when you are on the road, when you lie
down and when you rise up. You must tie them on
your hands as a memento, and wear them on your
forehead as a badge; you must inscribe them on the
door-posts of your houses and on your gates.

JOSHUA 1:8
8   This book of the law shall not depart out of thy
mouth; but thou shalt meditate therein day and
night, that thou mayest observe to do according to
all that is written therein: for then thou shalt

make thy way prosperous, and then thou shalt have good success.

JOSHUA 1:8 (*Berkeley*)
This book of the Law must never depart from your mouth; you must meditate on it day and night, so that you may keep living in accord with all that is written in it; for then you will make your way successful, and then you will prosper.

PSALM 119:54
54 Thy statutes have been my songs in the house of my pilgrimage.

PSALM 119:54 (*Basic English*)
Your rules have been melodies to me, while I have been living in strange lands.

PSALM 119:54 (*TLB*)
For these laws of yours have been my source of joy and singing through all these years of my earthly pilgrimage.

PSALM 119:54 (*AP*)
Your Word has been the source of all my singing while living here during this sojourn, waiting to go home.

LUKE 24:44,45
44 And he said unto them, These are the words which I spake unto you, while I was yet with you, that all things must be fulfilled, which were written in the law of Moses, and in the prophets, and in the psalms, concerning me.
45 Then opened he their understanding, that they might understand the scriptures.

LUKE 24:44,45 (*Phillips*)
Then he said, "Here and now are fulfilled the words that I told you when I was with you: that everything written about me in the Law of Moses and in the prophets and psalms must come true." Then he opened their minds so that they could understand the scriptures.

JOHN 14:21
21 He that hath my commandments, and keepeth them, he it is that loveth me: and he that loveth me shall be loved of my Father, and I will love him, and will manifest myself to him.

JOHN 14:21 (*Barclay*)
To know my commands and to obey them is really to love me. If anyone loves me, he will be loved by my Father, and I too will love him, and I will show myself clearly to him.

JOHN 14:21 (*Templeton*)
Prove your love for me by your obedience. Show your love for God and me and I'll return your love and reveal myself to you.

JOHN 14:23
23 Jesus answered and said unto him, If a man love me, he will keep my words: and my Father will love him, and we will come unto him, and make our abode with him.

JOHN 14:23 (*Godbey*)
Jesus responded and said to him; If any one may love me with divine love, he will keep my word: and my Father will love him, and we will come to him, and will make our mansion with him.

JOHN 14:23 (*Templeton*)
It stems from your love for me, he answered. Your obedience will bring you the Father's love and mine. We'll both share your daily life.

2 TIMOTHY 2:15
15 Study to shew thyself approved unto God, a workman that needeth not to be ashamed, rightly dividing the word of truth.

2 TIMOTHY 2:15 (*NIV*)
Do your best to present yourself to God as one approved, a workman who does not need to be ashamed and who correctly handles the word of truth.

2 TIMOTHY 2:15 (*Weymouth*)
Earnestly seek to commend yourself to God as a servant who, because of his straightforward dealing

with the word of truth, has no reason to feel any shame.

2 TIMOTHY 4:2
2   Preach the word; be instant in season, out of season; reprove, rebuke, exhort with all longsuffering and doctrine.

2 TIMOTHY 4:2 (*NIV*)
Preach the Word; be prepared in season and out of season; correct, rebuke and encourage with great patience and careful instruction.

HEBREWS 2:1
1   Therefore we ought to give the more earnest heed to the things which we have heard, lest at any time we should let them slip.

HEBREWS 2:1 (*Barclay*)
It is therefore necessary that we should pay all the more attention to what we have been told. Otherwise, we may well be like a ship which drifts past the harbour to shipwreck.

JAMES 1:22
22 But be ye doers of the word, and not hearers only, deceiving your own selves.

JAMES 1:22 (*Weymouth*)
But prove yourselves obedient to the Message, and do not be mere hearers of it, imposing a delusion upon yourselves.

Who Can Understand the Word of God?

JOHN 3:20,21
20 For every one that doeth evil hateth the light, neither cometh to the light, lest his deeds should be reproved.
21 But he that doeth truth cometh to the light, that his deeds may be made manifest, that they are wrought in God.

JOHN 3:20,21 (*Crofts*)
For every wrongdoer hates the light: he avoids it lest his deed be shown up. But those who act

uprightly come to the light, to show that their acts
have been inspired by God.

JOHN 3:20,21 (*Leo Tolstoy*)[1]
He who does wrong does not go to the light, so that
his deeds may not be seen, and such a one
bereaves himself of life. Whereas he who lives the
truth comes to the light, that his deeds are seen;
and he has life, and is united with God.

JOHN 4:23,24
23 But the hour cometh, and now is, when the true
worshippers shall worship the Father in spirit and
in truth: for the Father seeketh such to worship
him.
24 God is a Spirit: and they that worship him must
worship him in spirit and in truth.

JOHN 4:23,24 (*Blackwelder*)
Yes, the hour is coming, and now is, when the true
worshippers will worship the Father in spirit and
in truth. Indeed, the Father is searching for such
persons to worship Him. God in His essential
nature is spirit, and those who worship [Him]
must worship in spirit and in truth.

JOHN 4:23,24 (*Crofts*)
The time is coming — indeed it has already arrived —
when all genuine worshippers will worship the
Father spiritually and with utter sincerity. These are
the worshippers the Father wants. For God is a
Spirit, and those who worship him must do so spiritually and with utter sincerity.

JOHN 7:17
17 If any man will do his will, he shall know of the
doctrine, whether it be of God, or whether I speak
of myself.

JOHN 7:17 (*Noli*)
Anyone who desires to do his will can tell whether
my doctrine comes from God, or whether I am
teaching it on my own authority.

JOHN 7:17 *(Crofts)*
If anyone resolves firmly to do God's will, he'll
come to know beyond any doubt whether my doctrine is from God or whether I speak on my own
authority.

JOHN 8:43
43 Why do ye not understand my speech? even
because ye cannot hear my word.

JOHN 8:43 *(Crofts)*
Why is that you can't accept my teaching? I'll tell
you: it's because of your moral character.

JOHN 8:43 *(Riggs)*
Why is it that ye cannot perceive the divine accent
in all my speech? I will tell you. It is because you
cannot really hear my teaching; you are spiritually deaf to my message; morally incapable of understanding it.

JOHN 8:47
47 He that is of God heareth God's words: ye therefore hear them not, because ye are not of God.

JOHN 8:47 *(Riggs)*
It is a fact of experience that the spiritual within a
man reveals the spiritual outside of him; he who is
in fellowship with God as his child hears the words
of God. Herein is the cause of your dullness of hearing. Ye are not the children of God.

1 CORINTHIANS 2:12-15
12 Now we have received, not the spirit of the
world, but the spirit which is of God; that we might
know the things that are freely given to us of God.
13 Which things also we speak, not in the words
which man's wisdom teacheth, but which the Holy
Ghost teacheth; comparing spiritual things with
spiritual.
14 But the natural man receiveth not the things of
the Spirit of God: for they are foolishness unto
him: neither can he know them, because they are
spiritually discerned.
15 But he that is spiritual judgeth all things, yet
he himself is judged of no man.

1 CORINTHIANS 2:12-15 (*Shuttleworth*)
Now we have received, not the fallible spirit of this world, but the direct communications of that all-seeing divine Spirit, so that to us is given to know the operations of God's mercy, as extended to us and to mankind. And it is those divine communications which we now preach to the world, not in the artificial language of human wisdom, but as they are suggested to us by the Holy Spirit itself, expounding spiritual things in spiritual language. But the mere natural man apprehends not the revelations made by the Spirit of God, so as to be able to form a right judgment respecting them; for to him they are foolishness, because he judges of them carnally and not spiritually. He, on the contrary, who is illuminated by the gifts of the divine Spirit loses none of the natural knowledge which he previously possessed, but has a due perception of the things both of the spiritual and carnal world; but the carnal world, on the other hand, judges not him.

2 CORINTHIANS 4:3,4
3   But if our gospel be hid, it is hid to them that are lost:
4   In whom the god of this world hath blinded the minds of them which believe not, lest the light of the glorious gospel of Christ, who is the image of God, should shine unto them.

2 CORINTHIANS 4:3,4 (*Baxter*)
So that if our preaching be not yet understood and believed, it is not for want of our clear delivery, but from the miserable case of lost uncapable hearers. Because the devil, by the love of worldly things, ruling the hearts of worldly men, hath blinded them, that they may not believe the gospel, and see that glory which shineth in Christ, who is the image of God.

2 CORINTHIANS 4:3,4 (*Ben Campbell Johnson*)
If some do not perceive the Good news, it is those who have not opened themselves to reality. These persons have become insensitive because of their

choices to fulfill themselves through the worship
of the temporal creations of this age. So they do
not perceive the image of the eternal God who is
represented in Christ.

1 JOHN 2:20
20 But ye have an unction from the Holy One, and
ye know all things.

1 JOHN 2:20 (*Shuttleworth*)
You however have received enough of the assisting
communications of the Holy Spirit to be in no danger of being misled by their deceitful doctrines.

1 JOHN 2:20 (*Baxter*)
But the most holy God and Saviour hath anointed
you with his holy Spirit, which will lead you from
pernicious error, into all necessary truth, if you
obey him.

1 JOHN 2:27
27 But the anointing which ye have received of
him abideth in you, and ye need not that any man
teach you: but as the same anointing teacheth you
of all things, and is truth, and is no lie, and even as
it hath taught you, ye shall abide in him.

1 JOHN 2:27 (*Wand*)
The anointing with His Spirit, which you received
from Him, gives you instruction on every point, and
it is truth and not falsehood. Remain then firm in
fellowship with Him as His Spirit has taught you.

What the Bible Reveals of God
And His Character

GENESIS 1:1
1   In the beginning God created the heaven and
the earth.

GENESIS 1:1 (*Knox*)
God, at the beginning of time, created heaven and
earth.

EXODUS 15:11-13
11 Who is like unto thee, O Lord among the gods?
who is like thee, glorious in holiness, fearful in
praises, doing wonders?
12 Thou stretchedst out thy right hand, the earth
swallowed them.
13 Thou in thy mercy hast led forth the people
which thou hast redeemed: thou hast guided them
in thy strength unto thy holy habitation.

EXODUS 15:11-13 (*TLB*)
Who else is like the Lord among the gods? Who is
glorious in holiness like him? Who is so awesome
in splendor, A wonder-working God? You reached
out your hand and the earth swallowed them. You
have led the people you redeemed. But in your lov-
ingkindness You have guided them wonderfully to
your holy land.

EXODUS 15:11-13 (*NIV*)
Who among the gods is like you, O Lord? Who is
like you — majestic in holiness, awesome in glory,
working wonders? You stretched out your right
hand and the earth swallowed them. In your
unfailing love you will lead the people you have
redeemed. In your strength you will guide them to
your holy dwelling.

LEVITICUS 26:12
12 And I will walk among you, and will be your
God, and ye shall be my people.

LEVITICUS 26:12 (*Berkeley*)
I will be walking in your midst; I will be your God
and you will be My people.

PSALM 9:9,10
9 The Lord also will be a refuge for the
oppressed, a refuge in times of trouble.
10 And they that know thy name will put their
trust in thee: for thou, Lord, hast not forsaken
them that seek thee.

PSALM 9:9,10 (*Revised Psalter*)
The Lord also will be a defense for the oppressed: even a refuge in the time of trouble. And they that heed thy name will put their trust in thee: for thou Lord hast never failed them that seek thee.

PSALM 9:9,10 (*Noli*)
He'll deliver the oppressed, he will comfort the distressed; those who know your mercy, Lord, will trust you for you don't forsake your friends who love you.

PSALM 18:1-3
1   I will love thee, O Lord, my strength.
2   The Lord is my rock, and my fortress, and my deliverer, my God, my strength, in whom I will trust; my buckler, and the horn of my salvation, and my high tower.
3   I will call upon the Lord, who is worthy to be praised: so shall I be saved from mine enemies.

PSALM 18:1-3 (*McFadyen*)
With my whole soul I love Thee, O Lord, my strength. The Lord is my rock, my fortress, deliverer, my God, my rock, whereon I take refuge, my shield, my defender, my saviour, my tower, my refuge, my saviour, who saves me from violence. Worthy of praise is the Lord whom I call on, for He is my Saviour from all my foes.

PSALM 18:1-3 (*Noli*)
Lord, I love you, for you give me strength, Lord, my rock, my fort, my liberator, Lord, my shield, Almighty Savior! Praise the Lord! I shout and I exclaim, for he rescued me from all my foes.

PSALM 27:1
1   The Lord is my light and my salvation; whom shall I fear? the Lord is the strength of my life; of whom shall I be afraid?

PSALM 27:1 (*Moffatt*)
The Eternal is my light and aid; whom shall I fear? The Eternal is the fortress of my life; whom shall I dread?

PSALM 27:1 (*Lattey*)
Jehovah is my light and my salvation: of whom
shall I be afraid? Jehovah is the protection of my
life: of whom shall I be in dread?

PSALM 28:7
7   The Lord is my strength and my shield; my
heart trusted in him, and I am helped: therefore
my heart greatly rejoiceth; and with my song will
I praise him.

PSALM 28:7 (*Good News*)
The Lord protects and defends me; I trust in him.
He gives me help and makes me glad; I praise him
with joyful songs.

PSALM 28:7 (*Moffatt*)
The Eternal is my strength and shield, my heart
has faith in him; so I am helped, my heart exults
and I sing to his praise.

PSALM 32:7
7   Thou art my hiding place; thou shalt preserve
me from trouble; thou shalt compass me about
with songs of deliverance. Selah.

PSALM 32:7 (*Callan*)
Thou art my refuge from the trouble that besets
me; Thou art my joy; O save me from them that
encompass me!

PSALM 32:7 (*Rotherham*)
Thou art a hiding-place for me, from distress wilt
thou preserve me — with shouts of deliverance
wilt thou compass me about. Selah.

PSALM 33:18-21
18 Behold, the eye of the Lord is upon them that
fear him, upon them that hope in his mercy;
19 To deliver their soul from death, and to keep
them alive in famine.
20 Our soul waiteth for the Lord: he is our help
and our shield.

21 For our heart shall rejoice in him, because we
have trusted in his holy name.

PSALM 33:18-21 (*TLB*)
But the eyes of the Lord are watching over those
who fear him, who rely upon his steady love. He
will keep them from death even in times of famine!
We depend upon the Lord alone to save us. Only he
can help us; he protects us like a shield. No wonder
we are happy in the Lord! For we are trusting him.
We trust his holy name. Yes, Lord, let your constant
love surround us, for our hopes are in you alone.

PSALM 34:8
8   O taste and see that the Lord is good: blessed is
the man that trusteth in him.

PSALM 34:8 (*Noli*)
Try the Lord, and you will find him kind; blest is
he who asks for his protection.

PSALM 34:8 (*Zerr*)
Taste and eat your fill! How good Yahweh is! How
happy the man who takes shelter in him.

PSALM 34:17,18
17 The righteous cry, and the Lord heareth, and
delivereth them out of all their troubles.
18 The Lord is nigh unto them that are of a broken
heart; and saveth such as be of a contrite spirit.

PSALM 34:17,18 (*Callan*)
The just have cried, and the Lord has answered
them, delivering them from all their distresses.
The Lord is near to the broken in heart, and the
crushed in spirit He saves.

PSALM 91:1-4
1   He that dwelleth in the secret place of the most
High shall abide under the shadow of the
Almighty.
2   I will say of the Lord, He is my refuge and my
fortress: my God; in him will I trust.

3   Surely he shall deliver thee from the snare of the fowler, and from the noisome pestilence.
4   He shall cover thee with his feathers, and under his wings shalt thou trust: his truth shall be thy shield and buckler.

PSALM 91:1-4 (*Zerr*)

Whoever dwells in the shelter of the Most High and passes the night in the shadow of the Almighty — he says: "O Yahweh, my refuge, my stronghold, I put all my trust in you, my God." He alone will set you free from the snare; he alone will shield you from poisoned arrows. He will conceal you with his wings and under their shadow you will find refuge; his arm will be your shield and shelter.

PSALM 111:2-9

2   The works of the Lord are great, sought out of all them that have pleasure therein.
3   His work is honourable and glorious: and his righteousness endureth for ever.
4   He hath made his wonderful works to be remembered: the Lord is gracious and full of compassion.
5   He hath given meat unto them that fear him: he will ever be mindful of his covenant.
6   He hath shewed his people the power of his works, that he may give them the heritage of the heathen.
7   The works of his hands are verity and judgment; all his commandments are sure.
8   They stand fast for ever and ever, and are done in truth and uprightness.
9   He sent redemption unto his people: he hath commanded his covenant for ever: holy and reverend is his name.

PSALM 111:2-9 (*NIV*)

Great are the works of the Lord; they are pondered by all who delight in them. Glorious and majestic are his deeds, and his righteousness endures forever. He has caused his wonders to be remembered; the Lord is gracious and compassionate. He provides food for those who fear him; he remembers his covenant forever. He has shown his people the power of his works, giving them the lands of other nations. The works of his hands are faithful and just; all his precepts are trustworthy. They are steadfast for ever and ever, done in faithfulness and uprightness. He provided redemption for his people; he ordained his covenant forever — holy and awesome is his name.

PSALM 111:2-9 (*Noli*)
Mighty are the works of God, seek them, ponder them, delight in them; splendid, glorious are his achievements, everlasting is his righteousness. Celebrate on Sabbath days his triumphs, think of his compassion and his mercy; he has fed his worshippers, he has kept his covenants; his successes proved his power, he has given us the promised land, he is faithful, he is just, all his precepts are trustworthy; he's reliable forever, he is truthful and upright; he has granted freedom to his people and confirmed it with his covenant; holy, awesome is his Name forever!

PSALM 118:6
6   The Lord is on my side; I will not fear: what can man do unto me?

PSALM 118:6 (*Callan*)
The Lord is my helper; I shall not fear what man may do to me.

PSALM 118:6 (*Noli*)
God is on my side, I will not fear, no man can do any harm to me.

PSALM 118:6 (*Grimes*)
The Lord is with me, he will not forget that he has made me; why then should I fear?

PSALM 139:7,8
7   Whither shall I go from thy spirit? or whither shall I flee from thy presence?

8   If I ascend up into heaven, thou art there: if I
make my bed in hell, behold, thou art there.

PSALM 139:7,8 (*Moffatt*)
Where could I go from thy Spirit, where could I
flee from thy face? I climb to heaven — but thou
art there; I nestle in the nether-world — and there
thou art!

PSALM 139:7,8 (*Harrison*)
To what place shall I withdraw from Your influence? Where shall I retreat from Your presence? If
I ascend heavenward, You are there; if I make my
bed in hell, You are there also.

ISAIAH 6:3
3   And one cried unto another, and said, Holy,
holy, holy, is the Lord of hosts: the whole earth is
full of his glory.

ISAIAH 6:3 (*Moffatt*)
They kept calling to one another, "Holy, holy, holy,
is the Lord of hosts, his majestic splendour fills the
whole earth!"

ISAIAH 6:3 (*New Life*)
One called out to another and said, "Holy, holy,
holy, is the Lord of All. The whole earth is full of
His shining greatness."

ISAIAH 49:14-16
14   But Zion said, The Lord hath forsaken me, and
my Lord hath forgotten me.
15   Can a woman forget her sucking child, that she
should not have compassion on the son of her
womb? yea, they may forget, yet will I not forget
thee.
16   Behold, I have graven thee upon the palms of
my hands; thy walls are continually before me.

ISAIAH 49:14-16 (*Basic English*)
But Zion said, The Lord has given me up, I have
gone from His memory. Will a woman give up the
child at her breast, will she be without pity for the

fruit of her body? yes, these may, but I will not let
you go out of my memory. See, your name is marked
on my hands; your walls are ever before me.

ISAIAH 57:15
15 For thus saith the high and lofty One that inhab-
iteth eternity, whose name is Holy; I dwell in the
high and holy place, with him also that is of a contrite and humble spirit, to revive the spirit of the
humble, and to revive the heart of the contrite ones.

ISAIAH 57:15 (*Moffatt*)
For he who is high and uplifted, the Majestic One,
he who sits enthroned for ever, declares: "I sit on
high, enthroned, the Majestic One, and I am with
the crushed and humbled soul, to revive the spirit
of the humble, and to put heart into the crushed."

ISAIAH 57:15 (*Good News*)
I am the high and holy God, who lives forever. I
live in a high and holy place, but I also live with
people who are humble and repentant, so that I
can restore their confidence and hope.

JOHN 1:1-3
1 In the beginning was the Word, and the Word
was with God, and the Word was God.
2 The same was in the beginning with God.
3 All things were made by him; and without him
was not any thing made that was made.

JOHN 1:1-3 (*Parker*)
In the unbeginning was the Divine Being called
"The Logos" or the "The Word." He was the expres-
sion and the expresser of the thought of the triune
God. He was with God. He was God. He ever was
God. He was in and with God from the Unbeginning
beginning. Everything was originally made by
Him — He spoke and immediately forces and
things existed. Apart from Him nothing was
created.

JOHN 1:1-3 (*Moffatt*)
The Logos existed in the very beginning, the Logos
was with God, the Logos was divine. He was with

God in the very beginning: through him all existence came into being, no existence came into
being apart from him.

1 CORINTHIANS 1:9
9   God is faithful, by whom ye were called unto
the fellowship of his Son Jesus Christ our Lord.

1 CORINTHIANS 1:9 (*Shuttleworth*)
Meanwhile be assured, that God by whom you
were called to a participation in the redemption of
his Son Jesus Christ our Lord, will not recede from
his covenant which he has made with you.

1 CORINTHIANS 1:9 (*Baxter*)
For God is faithful, who freely called you to the
state of communion with and in Christ, when you
were aliens to it, and therefore will not fail you
when you are called and reconciled.

1 TIMOTHY 2:4
4   Who will have all men to be saved, and to come
unto the knowledge of the truth.

1 TIMOTHY 2:4 (*Tomanek*)
Who wishes all men to be saved and to come to an
exact knowledge of the truth.

1 TIMOTHY 2:4 (*Pyle*)
Thus extensive ought our Christian prayers to be;
since God never intended to exclude any part of
mankind from his providence and protection; but
especially not from the mercies of the Christian
covenant; but is desirous to have all nations enjoy
them, upon their acceptance of the faith, and obedience to the precepts of the gospel.

HEBREWS 8:10,11
10 For this is the covenant that I will make with
the house of Israel after those days, saith the Lord;
I will put my laws into their mind, and write them
in their hearts: and I will be to them a God, and
they shall be to me a people:

11 And they shall not teach every man his neigh-
bour, and every man his brother, saying, Know the
Lord: for all shall know me, from the least to the
greatest.

HEBREWS 8:10,11 (*Parker*)

For in the new covenant I promised to make with
the whole house of Israel, after the old covenant had
completely come to an end, there were these promises; I will put My laws into the book of their mind
and write them upon the fleshly tables of the heart,
and I will be a happy God unto them and they shall
be a happy people unto Me. Not again will I depend
upon the words of the law being written in a paper
book or on tables of stone. Then they shall not seek
to teach their neighbours and relatives to know the
Lord, for there will be no need of teaching, there
will be the inner revelation, and the youngest and
the oldest will spontaneously know Me.

HEBREWS 13:5,6

5   Let your conversation be without covetousness; and be content with such things as ye have:
for he hath said, I will never leave thee, nor forsake thee.
6   So that we may boldly say, The Lord is my helper,
and I will not fear what man shall do unto me.

HEBREWS 13:5,6 (*Peirce*)

Let your conversation and manner of life be free
from a greedy desire of the riches of this world, and
be contented with such things as you already enjoy,
so far as not to seek more with anxiety, or in any
unlawful way: since God will take care of you, and
says to you as he formerly said to other good men,
I will never leave thee, nor forsake thee. On which
account we may say with courage as the Psalmist
does, The Lord is continually my helper; and I will
not fear what any man shall, or is able to, do to me.

2 PETER 3:9

9   The Lord is not slack concerning his promise,
as some men count slackness; but is longsuffering

to us-ward, not willing that any should perish, but that all should come to repentance.

2 PETER 3:9 (*Shuttleworth*)
If the Lord appears at this moment slow to execute his judgments, it is not a slowness which proceeds from want of power, but from want of will; from his patient long-suffering; from his suspending again and again the day of his visitation, in the still lingering hope that none should finally perish, but that all may come to repentance.

2 PETER 3:9 (*Noli*)
Moreover, the Lord does not delay his promise, as some men think. He is really showing his patience with you, because he does not want any men to perish. On the contrary, he wants them all to come to repentance.

1 JOHN 1:7
7   But if we walk in the light, as he is in the light, we have fellowship one with another, and the blood of Jesus Christ his Son cleanseth us from all sin.

1 JOHN 1:7 (*Baxter*)
But if we walk in the light of holy knowledge, faith and purity, we have mutual communion with God, and with his Son Jesus Christ, whose blood doth cleanse us from all sin.

1 JOHN 1:7 (*Letters to Street Christians*)
But if we're living in God's perfect light, we are knit together in common vibrations of joy and the lifeblood of Jesus Himself washes away all of our selfish acts — past, present, and future.

Giving God's Word Top Priority in Your Life

EXODUS 24:3
3   And Moses came and told the people all the words of the Lord, and all the judgments: and all the people answered with one voice, and said, All the words which the Lord hath said will we do.

EXODUS 24:3 (*Good News*)
Moses went and told the people all the Lord's commands and all the ordinances, and all the people answered together, "We will do everything that the Lord has said."

DEUTERONOMY 4:2
2   Ye shall not add unto the word which I command you, neither shall ye diminish ought from it, that ye may keep the commandments of the Lord your God which I command you.

DEUTERONOMY 4:2 (*TLB*)
Do not add other laws or subtract from these; just obey them, for they are from the Lord your God.

DEUTERONOMY 6:6
6   And these words, which I command thee this day, shall be in thine heart.

DEUTERONOMY 6:6 (*Good News*)
Never forget these commands that I am giving you today.

DEUTERONOMY 6:6 (*Basic English*)
Keep these words, which I say to you this day, deep in your hearts.

DEUTERONOMY 8:3
3   And he humbled thee, and suffered thee to hunger, and fed thee with manna, which thou knewest not, neither did thy fathers know; that he might make thee know that man doth not live by bread only, but by every word that proceedeth out of the mouth of the Lord doth man live.

DEUTERONOMY 8:3 (*TLB*)
Yes, he humbled you by letting you go hungry and then feeding you with manna, a food previously unknown to both you and your ancestors. He did it to help you realize that food isn't everything, and that real life comes by obeying every command of God.

DEUTERONOMY 30:14
14 But the word is very nigh unto thee, in thy mouth, and in thy heart, that thou mayest do it.

DEUTERONOMY 30:14 (*New Life*)
But the Word is very near you, in your mouth and in your heart, so that you may obey it.

DEUTERONOMY 30:14 (*Knox*)
No, this message of mine is close to thy side; it rises to thy lips, it is printed on thy memory; thou hast only to fulfil it.

JOSHUA 1:8
8   This book of the law shall not depart out of thy mouth; but thou shalt meditate therein day and night, that thou mayest observe to do according to all that is written therein: for then thou shalt make thy way prosperous, and then thou shalt have good success.

JOSHUA 1:8 (*Beck*)
Don't stop reading this book of the Law, but day and night think of what it says, so you can be careful to do everything written in it; then you will prosper and succeed.

JOSHUA 1:8 (*New Life*)
This book of the Law must not leave your mouth. Think about it day and night, so you may be careful to do all that is written in it. Then all will go well with you. You will receive many good things.

1 CHRONICLES 16:15
15 Be ye mindful always of his covenant; the word which he commanded to a thousand generations;

1 CHRONICLES 16:15 (*Knox*)
Keep in everlasting memory that covenant of his, that promise bequeathed to a thousand coming generations.

1 CHRONICLES 16:15 (*Good News*)
Never forget God's covenant, which he made to last forever.

JOB 22:22
22 Receive, I pray thee, the law from his mouth, and lay up his words in thine heart.

JOB 22:22 (*Beck*)
Let Him teach you, and what He says treasure in your mind.

JOB 22:22 (*Knox*)
Let his lips be thy oracle, his words written on thy heart.

JOB 23:12
12 Neither have I gone back from the commandment of his lips; I have esteemed the words of his mouth more than my necessary food.

JOB 23:12 (*Good News*)
I always do what God commands; I follow his will, not my own desires.

JOB 23:12 (*Basic English*)
I have never gone against the orders of his lips; the words of his mouth have been stored up in my heart.

JOB 23:12 (*New Life*)
I have not turned away from the words of His lips. I have stored up the words of His mouth. They are worth more to me than the food I need.

PSALM 19:7
7   The law of the Lord is perfect, converting the soul: the testimony of the Lord is sure, making wise the simple.

PSALM 19:7 (*Beck*)
The Lord's word is perfect and gives new life. The Lord's truth can be trusted to make simple people wise.

PSALM 19:7 (*New Life*)
The Law of the Lord is perfect, giving new strength to the soul. The Law He has made known is sure, making the child-like wise.

PSALM 37:30,31
30 The mouth of the righteous speaketh wisdom,
and his tongue talketh of judgment.
31 The law of his God is in his heart; none of his
steps shall slide.

PSALM 37:30,31 (*Good News*)
A good man's words are wise, and he is always fair.
He keeps the law of his God in his heart and never
departs from it.

PSALM 37:30,31 (*Knox*)
Right reason is on the good man's lips, well
weighed are all his counsels; his steps never falter,
because the law of God rules in his heart.

PSALM 119:9
9 Wherewithal shall a young man cleanse his
way? by taking heed thereto according to thy word.

PSALM 119:9 (*RSV*)
How can a young man keep his way pure? By
guarding it according to thy word.

PSALM 119:9 (*Zerr*)
How can a young man keep himself pure? By
maintaining his paths according to your word.

PSALM 119:9 (*Beck*)
How can a young man keep his life pure? By living
as You tell him to.

ISAIAH 40:8
8 The grass withereth, the flower fadeth: but the
word of our God shall stand for ever.

ISAIAH 40:8 (*Basic English*)
The grass is dry, the flower is dead; but the word of
our God is eternal.

MATTHEW 7:24,25
24 Therefore whosoever heareth these sayings of
mine, and doeth them, I will liken him unto a wise
man, which built his house upon a rock:

25 And the rain descended, and the floods came,
and the winds blew, and beat upon that house; and
it fell not: for it was founded upon a rock.

MATTHEW 7:24,25 (*Templeton*)
Those who practice what I preach show the same
kind of sense as the man who excavated until he
struck rock and then laid the foundation for his
house on that rock. Later, a violent storm came up,
and although the flood waters swept against the
house and the winds howled about it, it stood
unshaken. It had been well built on a solid foundation. Those who pay no attention to what I say are
as foolish as the man who was indifferent to the
need for a solid foundation and built his house on
sand. When the storm came, his house was swept
away and wrecked.

MARK 13:31
31 Heaven and earth shall pass away: but my
words shall not pass away.

MARK 13:31 (*Johnson*)
Everything else in this world may become null and
void, but the truth I declare will not; it will stand.

The Divine Authority of God's Word

PSALM 33:6
6   By the word of the Lord were the heavens made;
and all the host of them by the breath of his mouth.

PSALM 33:6 (*Zerr*)
At the word of Yahweh the heavens were made; a
breath of his created all the lights that are in them.

PSALM 33:6 (*Noli*)
With an order he created heavens, with a word the
stars which cover them.

PSALM 33:6 (*Good News*)
The Lord created the heavens by his command, the
sun, moon, and stars by his spoken word.

PSALM 33:9
9   For he spake, and it was done; he commanded, and it stood fast.

PSALM 33:9 (*Callan*)
For He spoke, and they sprang into being; He commanded, and they were made.

PSALM 119:89
89 For ever, O Lord, thy word is settled in heaven.

PSALM 119:89 (*Noli*)
Lord, your Scriptures are eternal and unshakable they stand in heaven.

PSALM 119:89 (*Lattey*)
Thy word, Jehovah is fixed in heaven for ever.

PROVERBS 30:5
5   Every word of God is pure: he is a shield unto them that put their trust in him.

PROVERBS 30:5 (*Beck*)
Everything God said has proved to be true. He's a Shield to those who come to Him for protection.

ISAIAH 55:10,11
10 For as the rain cometh down, and the snow from heaven, and returneth not thither, but watereth the earth, and maketh it bring forth and bud, that it may give seed to the sower, and bread to the eater:
11 So shall my word be that goeth forth out of my mouth: it shall not return unto me void, but it shall accomplish that which I please, and it shall prosper in the thing whereto I sent it.

ISAIAH 55:10,11 (*New Life*)
The rain and snow come down from heaven and do not return there without giving water to the earth. This makes plants grow on the earth, and gives seeds to the planter and bread to the eater. So My

Word which goes from My mouth will not return to
Me empty. It will do what I want it to do, and will
carry out My plan well.

ISAIAH 55:10,11 (*NIV*)
As the rain and the snow come down from heaven,
and do not return to it without watering the earth
and making it bud and flourish, so that it yields
seed for the sower and bread for the eater, so is my
word that goes out from my mouth: it will not
return to me empty, but will accomplish what I
desire and achieve the purpose for which I sent it.

2 CORINTHIANS 1:20
20 For all the promises of God in him are yea, and
in him Amen, unto the glory of God by us.

2 CORINTHIANS 1:20 (*Johnson*)
Each of us affirmed that Jesus is God's yes to life.
Every promise God has made to us finds its fulfillment in Christ. He is God's consummate yes to
existence and the key to God's ultimate fulfillment
through us.

2 CORINTHIANS 1:20 (*Barclay*)
In him all God's promises find their yes. That is
why when to the glory of God we say "Amen" we say
it through him — "through Jesus Christ our Lord."

1 PETER 1:23-25
23 Being born again, not of corruptible seed, but
of incorruptible, by the word of God, which liveth
and abideth for ever.
24 For all flesh is as grass, and all the glory of man
as the flower of grass. The grass withereth, and the
flower thereof falleth away:
25 But the word of the Lord endureth for ever.
And this is the word which by the gospel is
preached unto you.

1 PETER 1:23-25 (*TLB*)
For you have a new life. It was not passed on to you
from your parents, for the life they gave you will

fade away. This new one will last forever, for it comes from Christ, God's ever-living Message to men. Yes, our natural lives will fade as grass does when it becomes all brown and dry. All our greatness is like a flower that droops and falls; but the Word of the Lord will last forever. And his message is the Good News that was preached to you.

1 PETER 1:23-25 (*Simple English*)
You have been born again. The seed that caused this will never die. It is God's message that lives and lasts. "All human flesh is like grass. Its glory is like a grass flower. The grass burns up and the flowers falls off, but the Lord's message remains forever." This is the message which was preached to you.

---

[1] Tolstoy wrote at least two works on the Gospels, *The Gospel in Brief* and *The Four Gospels Harmonized*. Both have been translated into English.

Conclusion

It was told to me once that while on his deathbed the late evangelist D. L. Moody was asked what, if anything, he would have done differently in his life and ministry. Although Rev. Moody was considered very knowledgeable concerning Scripture, his reply was that, if he could have done anything differently, he would have spent more time in the study of God's Word.

What Rev. Moody had come to know was that the vital link between God and man is the Bible. Within the pages of the Bible can be found the wisdom of God and the plan of the Lord for His children. God's Word is His will. It is the only spiritual food whereby we can grow and come to a deeper knowledge of Him.

As you begin expanding the boundaries of your study of God's Word, it is my prayer that you will find untold riches within its pages, riches to meet your every need. You will be able to draw information from *How To Study The Word* that will serve you for many years to come, as you continue expanding your horizons. Do not be afraid to use books, Bibles, and reference materials that you are at first unfamiliar with. Rather, view them as guides along the path of understanding.

Planting God's Word in your heart is the most important thing you will ever do for yourself. I urge you not to let anything come between you and your study of God's Word. Take advantage of all the wonderful Bible translations and study materials available to you. Experiment with various styles of Bible study until you find those that are right for you. But most importantly, however you do it, study God's Word, and it will grow in your heart and change your life!

Bibles Quoted

Adams, Jay E. *The Christian Counselor's New Testament:* Presbyterian and Reformed Publishing Co., 1977.

Anderson, H. T. *The New Testament Translated From the Original Greek.* Louisville, Ky: John P. Morton and Co., 1866.

Anderson, Julian G. *A New Accurate Translation of the Greek New Testament into Simple Everyday American English.* Naples, Fla.: Julian G. Anderson, 1984.

Ballantine, William G. *The Riverside New Testament. Rev.* ed. Boston: Houghton Mifflin Company, 1934.

Barclay, William. *The Daily Study Bible.* 1st ed. Philadelphia: The Westminster Press, 1958.

Barclay, William. *The New Testament: A New Translation.* New York: Collins, 1969.

Baxter, Richard. *A Paraphrase of the New Testament, with Notes, Doctrinal and Practical.* London: Richard Edwards, 1811.

Beck, William F. *The Holy Bible in the Language of Today: An American Translation.* Philadelphia: A. J. Holman Company, 1976.

Blackwelder, Boyce W. *The Four Gospels and Exegetical Translation.* Anderson, Ind.: Warner Press, 1980.

Bowes, John. *The New Testament Translated From the Purest Greek.* Dundee: John Bowes, 1870.

Brandt, Leslie F. *Psalms / Now.* St. Louis: Concordia Publishing House, 1973.

Callan, Charles J. *The Psalms Translated From the Latin Psalter.* New York: Joseph F. Wagner, Inc., 1944.

Cheyne, T .K. *The Book of Psalms.* London: Kegan Paul, Trench and Co., 1884.

Conybeare, W. J. *The Epistles of Paul.* Grand Rapids: Baker Book House, 1958.

Cressman, Annie. *Good News for the World: The New Testament in Worldwide English.* Bombay: SOON! Publications, 1969.

Crofts, Freeman Wills. *The Four Gospels in One Story.* New York: Longmans, Green and Co., 1949.

Doddridge, Philip. *The Family Expositor or a Paraphrase and Version of the New Testament with Critical Notes.* London: Thomas Tegg, 1829.

Edington, Andrew. *The Word Made Fresh.* Atlanta: John Knox Press, 1975.

Fanchiotti, Margherita. *A Beginner's Bible.* New York: Oxford University Press, 1959.

Fenton, Ferrar. *The Holy Bible in Modern English.* 10th ed. Merrimac, Mass.: Destiny Publishers, 1966.

Fillion, L. C. *The New Psalter of the Roman Breviary Text and Translation.* 3rd ed. St. Louis: B. Herder, 1923.

Godbey, W. B. *Translation of the New Testament from the Original Greek.* Cincinnati: M.W. Knapp, n.d.

Goddard, Dwight. *The Good News Of a Spiritual Realm.* Rev. ed. Chicago: Fleming H. Revell Company, 1916.

Good News Bible / Today's English Version. New York: American Bible Society, 1976.

Green, Thomas Sheldon. *The Twofold New Testament.* London: Samuel Bagster and Sons, n.d.

Grimes, Willard M. *The Unquenched Cup.* New York: Lifetime Editions, 1948.

Hammond, Henry. *A Paraphrase and Annotations Upon all the Books of the New Testament.* 4th ed. London: Ric. Davis Bookseller, 1675.

Harrison, R. K. *The Psalms For Today.* Grand Rapids: Zondervan Publishing House, 1961.

Hayman, Henry. *Epistles of the New Testament. Tulsa:* Spirit to Spirit Publications, 1982.

Holy Bible, New International Version®. NIV®. Grand Rapids: Zondervan, 1973, 1978, 1984 by International Bible Society.

Hudson, James T. *The Epistle to the Hebrews: Its Meaning and Message.* Edinburgh: T & T Clark, 1937.

Hurault, Bernardo. *Christian Community Bible.* Pastoral ed. Manila, Philippines: Divine Word Publications, 1988.

Johnson, Ben Campbell. *Matthew and Mark: A Relational Paraphrase.* Waco, Tex.: Word Books, 1978.

Johnson, Ben Campbell. *The Heart of Paul.* Waco, Tex.: Word Books, 1976.

Jordan, Clarence. *The Cottonpatch Version of Matthew and John.* Chicago: Association Press, 1970.

Jordan, Clarence. *The Cotton Patch Version of Paul's Epistles.* Chicago: Association Press, 1968.

Kasemann, Ernst. *Commentary on Romans.* 4th ed. Grand Rapids: William B. Eerdmans Publishing Company, 1986.

Kent, Homer A. Jr. *The Pastoral Epistles.* Chicago: Moody Press. 1982.

Knoch, A. E. *Concordant Literal New Testament.* 6th ed. Canyon Country, Calif.: Concordant Publishing Concern, 1983.

Knox, Ronald A. Msgr. *The New Testament of Our Lord and Saviour Jesus Christ: A New Translation.* New York: Sheed and Ward, 1945.

Lattey, Cuthbert. *The Psalter in the Westminster Version of the Sacred Scriptures.* London: Sands and Co., 1944.

Laubach, Frank. *The Inspired Letters In Clearest English.* New York: Thomas Nelson and Sons, 1956.

Leadyard, Gleson. *Holy Bible: New Life Version.* Canby, Oregon: Christian Literature International, 1986.

Leeser, Isaac. *Twenty-Four Books of the Holy Scriptures.* New York: Hebrew Publishing Company, n.d.

Lovett, C.S. *Lovett's Lights on Acts.* Baldwin Park, Calif.: Personal Christianity, 1972.

MacFadyen, John Edgar. *The Psalms in Modern Speech and Rhythmical Form.* London: James Clarke and Co., 1916.

MacFadyen, John Edgar. *The Wisdom Books in Modern Speech and Rythinical Form.* 2nd ed. London: James Clarke and Co., n.d.

MacKnight, James. *A New Literal Translation From the Original Greek of All the Apostolical Epistles.* New ed. Grand Rapids: Baker Book House, 1969.

Matheny, C. Howard. *Good News From God: A Translation of John.* Columbia, S.C.: no. pub., 1984.

Moffatt, James. *A New Translation of The Bible Containing The Old and New Testaments.* London: Hodder and Stoughton Limited, n.d.

Moffatt, James. *The Historical New Testament.* 2nd ed. rev. Edinburgh: T & T Clark, 1901.

Montgomery, Helen Barrett. *Centenary Translation of the New Testament in Modern English.* Valley Forge: The Judson Press, 1968.

Moule, H. C. G. *Studies in II Timothy.* Grand Rapids: Kregel Publications, 1977.

Murdock, James. *The New Testament.* New York: Robert Carter and Brothers. 1859.

New American Standard Bible. Glendale, Calif.: Regal Books, 1971.

New Century Version. Fort Worth, Tex.: Sweet Publishing, 1984.

Newcome, William. *The New Testament in an Improved Version.* Boston: Thomas B. Wait and Company, 1809.

Noli, Metropolitan Fan S. *The New Testament of Our Lord and Saviour Jesus Christ.* Boston, Mass.: Albanian Orthodox Church in America, 1961.

Noli, Metropolitan Fan S. *The Psalms.* Boston: Albanian Orthodox Church in America, 1964.

Norlie, Olaf M. *Norlie's Simplified New Testament in Plain English for Today's Reader.* Grand Rapids: Zondervan Publishing House, 1961.

Parker, P. G. *The Clarified New Testament.* Lynton, Devon, England: The Christian Workers Bible Centre, n.d.

Peirce, James. *A Paraphrase and Notes on the Epistles of St. Paul to the Colossians, Philippians, and Hebrews.* 2nd ed. London: J. Noon, 1733.

Peterson, Eugene H. *The Message: The New Testament in Contemporary Language.* Colorado Springs: Navpress, 1993.

Phillips, J. B. *New Testament in Modern English.* New York: Macmillan Publishing Company, 1958.

Povah, J. W. *The Book of Hosea.* London: National Adult School Union, n.d.

Pyle, Thomas. *A paraphrase on the Acts of the Holy Apostles, and Upon All the Epistles of the New Testament.* London: Booksellers of Oxford, Cambridge, and London, 1795.

Richert, Ernest. *Freedom Dynamics.* Big Bear Lake, Calif.: The Thinker, 1977.

Riggs, James Stevenson. *The Messages of the Bible. The Messages Of Jesus According To The Gospel Of John.* New York: Charles Scribner's Sons, 1907.

Rotherham, Joseph Bryant. *The Emphasised Bible, A New Translation* 3rd ed. Cincinnati: Standard Publishing Company, 1897.

Rotherham, Joseph. *The New Testament Newly Translated From the Greek Text of Tregelles and Critically Emphasised. 2nd* ed. rev. New York: John Wiley and Sons, 1890.

Rutherford, William Gunion. *Five Pauline Epistles A New Translation.* Malvern, Worcs. England: Golden Age Books, 1984.

Sawyer, Leicester Ambrose. *The New Testament. Boston:* John P. Jewett and Company, 1858.

Shuttleworth, Philip Nicholas. *A Paraphrastic Translation of the Apostolical Epistles with Notes.* 3rd ed. London: J. G. & F. Rivington, 1834.

Smith, J. M. Powis and Edgar J. Goodspeed. *The Bible: An American Translation.* Chicago: The University of Chicago Press, 1948.

Spurrell, Helen. *A Translation of the Old Testament Scriptures from the Original Hebrew.* London: James Nisbet & Co., 1885.

Swann, George. *New Testament of our Lord and Saviour Jesus Christ.* 4th ed. Robards, Ky.: George Swann Company, 1947.

Templeton, Charles B. *Jesus . . . The Four Gospels Rendered in Modern English*. New York: Simon and Schuster, 1973.

The Amplified New Testament. 19th ed. La Habra, Calif.: The Lockman Foundation, 1958.

The Bible in Basic English. Cambridge: Evans Brothers, LTD, 1965.

The Geneva Bible, The Annotated New Testament. 1602 ed. New York: The Pilgrim Press, 1989.

The Holy Bible: American Standard Version. 1901 ed. Nashville: Thomas Nelson Publishers, 1929 by International Council of Religious Education.

The Holy Bible: Revised Standard Version. Philadelphia: A. J. Holman Company, 1962.

The Holy Bible: Revised Version. New York: Oxford University Press, 1898.

The Holy Bible: The Berkeley Version in Modern English. Grand Rapids: Zondervan Publishing House, 1959.

The Holy Bible Newly Edited by the American Revision Committee. Nashville: Thomas Nelson, Publishers, 1901. (This is the *American Standard Version*.)

The Modern Language New Testament (The New Berkeley Version). Grand Rapids: Zondervan Publishing House, 1970.

The New English Bible New Testament. Cambridge: Cambridge University Press. 1961.

The New Testament of the New Jerusalem Bible. New York: Image Books, 1986.

The Revised Psalter. London: S.P.C.K., 1964.

The Simple English Bible. American ed. New York: International Bible Publishing Company, 1981.

The Living Bible. Wheaton, Ill.: Tyndale House Publishers, 1971.

The Translator's New Testament. London: The British and Foreign Bible Society, 1973.

The Twentieth Century New Testament — Revised Edition. Chicago: Fleming H. Revell Company, 1904.

The Twentieth Century New Testament — Tentative Edition Chicago: Fleming H. Revell Company, 1898.

Tolstoy, Leo. *A Confession, The Gospel in Brief and What I Believe*. Aylmer Maude, trans. London: Oxford University Press, 1974.

Tomanek, James L. *The New Testament of Our Lord and Savior Jesus Anointed*. Pocatello, Idaho: Arrowhead Press, 1958.

Two Brothers from Berkeley, *Letters to Street Christians*. Grand Rapids: Zondervan Publishing House, 1971.

Tyndale, William. *Tyndale's New Testament in a Modern-Spelling Edition*. David Daniell, ed. 1534 Edition, New Haven: Yale University Press, 1989.

Wade, G. W. *The Documents of The New Testament*. London: Thomas Murby and Co., 1934.

Wand, J. W. C. *The New Testament Letters*. New York: Oxford University Press, 1947.

Way, Arthur. *The Letters of St. Paul*. 8th ed. Chicago: Moody Press, 1950.

Weigle, Luther A., ed. *The New Testament Octapla*. New York: Thomas Nelson and Sons, 1950.

Wesley, John. *Explanatory Notes Upon the New Testament*. London: The Epworth Press, 1948.

Westcott, Brooke Foss. *Saint Paul's Epistle to the Ephesians*. Grand Rapids: Baker Book House, 1979.

Weymouth, Richard Francis. *The New Testament in Modern Speech*. 3rd ed. London: James Clarke and Co., 1909.

Williams, Charles B. *The New Testament: A Private Translation in the Language of the People*. Chicago: Moody Press, 1957.

Worrell, A. S. *The Worrell New Testament*. Springfield, Mo.: Gospel Publishing House, 1980.

Wuest, Kenneth S. *The New Testament: An Expanded Translation*. Grand Rapids, Mich.: William B. Eerdmans Publishing Company, 1961.

Wycliffe, John. *The New Testament in English 1388 Edition*. Oxford: Clarendon Press, 1879.

Young, Robert. *Young's Literal Translation of the Holy Bible*. 3rd. ed. Grand Rapids: Baker Book House, n.d.

Zerr, Bonaventure. *The Psalms, A New Translation*. New York: Paulist Press, 1979.

Bibliography

Austin-Sparks, T. *The Centrality and Universality of the Cross.* Washington, D.C.: Testimony Book Ministry, n.d.

Blaiklock, E. M. *Blaiklock's Handbook to the Bible.* Old Tappan, New Jersey: Fleming H. Revell Company, 1980.

Blair, Edward P. *Abingdon Bible Handbook.* Nashville: Abingdon Press, 1975.

Bullinger, Ethelbert W. *A Critical Lexicon and Concordance to the English and Greek New Testament.* Grand Rapids: Zondervan Publishing House, 1979.

Cohen, A. *The Psalms Hebrew Text, English Translation and Commentary.* Hindhead, Surrey, England: The Soncino Press, 1945.

Eerdman's Handbook to the Bible. David and Pat Alexander, eds. Grand Rapids: William B. Eerdman's Publishing Company, 1973.

Eerdman's Handbook to the History of Christianity. Tim Dowley, ed. Grand Rapids: William B. Eerdmans Publishing Co., 1977.

Foxe, John. *Foxe's Book of English Martyrs.* Waco, Tex.: Word Books, 1981.

Gesenius, William. *Gesenius' Hebrew and Chaldee Lexicon to the Old Testament Scriptures.* Grand Rapids: Baker Book House, 1979.

Goodrick, Edward W. and John R. Kohlenberger, III. *The NIV Complete Concordance.* Grand Rapids: Zondervan, 1981.

Goodspeed, Edgar J. *The Making of the New Testament.* Chicago: The University of Chicago Press, 1925.

Halley, Henry H. *Halley's Bible Handbook.* Grand Rapids: Zondervan Publishing House, 1965.

Herbert, A. S. *Historical Catalogue of Printed Editions of the English Bible, 1525-1961.* New York: The American Bible Society, n.d.

Henry, Matthew. *Matthew Henry's Commentary on the Whole Bible.* McLean, Va: MacDonald Publishing Company, n.d.

Jamieson, Fausset, and Brown. *A Commentary Critical and Explanatory on the Whole Bible.* Grand Rapids: William B. Eerdmans Publishing Co., 1945.

Kenyon, E. W. *The Blood Covenant.* Kenyon's Gospel Publishing Society, 1969.

Moody, D. L. *Pleasure and Profit in Bible Study.* Chicago: Moody Press, n.d.

Nave, Orville J. *Nave's Topical Bible.* Nashville: The Southwestern Company, 1962.

Newell, William R. *Hebrews Verse by Verse.* Chicago: Moody Press, 1947.

Newell, William R. *Romans Verse by Verse.* Chicago: Moody Press, 1938.

Newell, William R. *The Book of the Revelation.* Chicago: Moody Press, 1978.

Pick, Aaron. *Dictionary of Old Testament Words for English Readers.* Grand Rapids: Kregel Publications, 1979.

Strong, James. *The Exhaustive Concordance of the Bible.* Nashville: Abingdon Press, 1983.

Thayer, Joseph Henry. A *Greek-English Lexicon of New Testament.* Grand Rapids: Baker Book House, 1977.

The Bible Almanac. James I. Packer, Merrill C. Tenney and William White, Jr., eds. Nashville: Thomas Nelson Publishers, 1980.

The Book of Common Prayer. New York: The Church Pension Fund, 1945.

The New Testament from 26 Translations. Curtis Vaughan, ed. Grand Rapids: Zondervan Publishing House, 1967.

The Treasury of Scripture Knowledge. McLean, Va.: MacDonald Publishing Company, 1982.

Theological Wordbook of the Old Testament. R. Laird Harris, Gleason L. Archer, Jr. and Bruce K. Waltke, eds. Chicago: Moody Press, 1980.

Unger, Merrill F. *Unger's Bible Handbook.* 1st ed. Chicago: Moody Press, 1966.

Vine, W. E., Merrill F. Unger and William White Jr., *Vine's Expository Dictionary of Biblical Words.* Nashville: Thomas Nelson Publishers, 1985.

Wilson, William. *Old Testament Word Studies.* Grand Rapids: Kregel Publications, 1980.

Young, Robert. *Young's Analytical Concordance to the Bible.* Nashville: Thomas Nelson Publishers, 1970.

Zondervan. *The NASB Handy Concordance.* Grand Rapids, 1984.

Zondervan. *The RSV Handy Concordance.* Grand Rapids, n.d.

About The Author

Terry Lawson has felt the call of the Lord to be a teacher to the Body of Christ since early in his Christian life. To help him to prepare for this ministry, he began collecting and using Bible translations and other study books. He became interested in Bible translations through the ministry of Kenneth E. Hagin, listening to his broadcasts and reading his books. Terry soon developed a strong desire to understand the Bible for himself.

Today he has an extensive Christian library including more than 300 translations of the Bible in whole or in part. He gives classes and seminars on how to study the Bible, teaching Christians the material found in this book. He currently pastors Living Word Fellowship in Joplin, Missouri, where he lives with his wife and two children.

To contact the author, write:

Terry Lawson
P. O. Box 3423
Joplin, MO 64803

*Please include your prayer requests and
comments when you write.*